Approaches to Teaching Achebe's
Things Fall Apart

Approaches to Teaching
World Literature

Joseph Gibaldi, series editor

For a complete listing of titles,
see the last pages of this book.

Approaches to Teaching Achebe's *Things Fall Apart*

Edited by
Bernth Lindfors

The Modern Language Association of America
New York   1991

For information about obtaining permission to reprint material from
MLA book publications, send your request by mail (see address below),
e-mail (permissions@mla.org), or fax (212 477-9863).

Library of Congress Cataloging-in-Publication Data

Approaches to teaching Achebe's Things fall apart
/ edited by Bernth Lindfors.
p.   cm. —(Approaches to teaching world literature ; 37)
Includes bibliographical references and index.
ISBN 0-87352-547-7 (cloth) / ISBN 0-87352-548-5 (pbk.)
1. Achebe, Chinua. Things fall apart.   2. Achebe, Chinua—Study and teaching.
3. Igbo (African people) in literature.
I. Lindfors, Bernth.   II. Series.
PR9387.9.A3T5239   1991
823—dc20   91-26230
ISSN 1059-1133

Printed on recycled paper

Cover illustration of the paperback edition: Igbo carved funerary stone, Nigeria, from Geoffrey
Williams, *African Designs from Traditional Sources* (New York: Dover, 1971) 168.

Published by The Modern Language Association of America
10 Astor Place, New York, New York 10003-6981

CONTENTS

PREFACE TO THE SERIES

In *The Art of Teaching* Gilbert Highet wrote, "Bad teaching wastes a great deal of effort, and spoils many lives which might have been full of energy and happiness." All too many teachers have failed in their work, Highet argued, simply "because they have not thought about it." We hope that the Approaches to Teaching World Literature series, sponsored by the Modern Language Association's Publications Committee, will not only improve the craft—as well as the art—of teaching but also encourage serious and continuing discussion of the aims and methods of teaching literature.

The principal objective of the series is to collect within each volume different points of view on teaching a specific literary work, a literary tradition, or a writer widely taught at the undergraduate level. The preparation of each volume begins with a wide-ranging survey of instructors, thus enabling us to include in the volume the philosophies and approaches, thoughts and methods of scores of experienced teachers. The result is a sourcebook of material, information, and ideas on teaching the subject of the volume to undergraduates.

The series is intended to serve nonspecialists as well as specialists, inexperienced as well as experienced teachers, graduate students who wish to learn effective ways of teaching as well as senior professors who wish to compare their own approaches with the approaches of colleagues in other schools. Of course, no volume in the series can ever substitute for erudition, intelligence, creativity, and sensitivity in teaching. We hope merely that each book will point readers in useful directions; at most each will offer only a first step in the long journey to successful teaching.

Joseph Gibaldi
Series Editor

PREFACE TO THE VOLUME

Chinua Achebe's *Things Fall Apart* is Africa's most famous novel. Published in London in 1958, it is now read everywhere in the English-speaking world and has been translated into more than thirty Western and non-Western languages. Over three million copies have been sold. Few modern literary works achieve such impressive distribution and win universal critical acclaim. *Things Fall Apart* has already earned the status of a modern classic.

One measure of its high reputation is its regular adoption as a textbook in a variety of university and high school courses—everything from graduate seminars in English and comparative literature to undergraduate offerings in English, history, anthropology, folklore, political science, ethnic studies, and African studies to high school classes in literature and social studies. (I was delighted to find a chapter from it reproduced in my daughter's fifth-grade social studies reader in Austin, Texas.) So, in addition to its popular success, *Things Fall Apart* has received acclaim in the classroom, becoming a required text in many different academic settings.

Yet teaching such a book presents special problems. *Things Fall Apart* is rooted in African social realities that North Americans and Europeans tend to know very little about. Students may need basic background information to understand the significance of certain actions in the story, but where can a teacher acquire this kind of cultural expertise? It isn't merely a matter of learning ethnographic facts, for larger issues of interpretation depend on an awareness of what was happening in Africa at the time the novel was being written. What was Achebe trying to say, in the late 1950s, by telling a tale about the disintegration of traditional Igbo (Ibo) society in colonial Nigeria? Why did he choose as his hero an ambitious, brutal man who ultimately commits suicide? Why did he elect to write in English rather than in his native tongue? How faithful is the book to history? Teachers unacquainted with Africa's colonial past may find such questions difficult to answer and may need to do some homework before plunging into this book with their students.

The essays collected here offer approaches to teaching an unfamiliar and multifaceted novel. On the surface, *Things Fall Apart* may seem a simple, uncomplicated story, but it has subtle and profound dimensions that those coming to it for the first time might easily miss. The authors of these essays, in addition to providing sound pedagogical advice, have attempted to help teachers recognize the rich complexity of this extraordinary novel. Readers will find both information and interpretation: some contributions place the tale in a meaningful sociocultural, historical, or aesthetic context while others focus primarily on exegetical or hermeneutical matters, sometimes considering little outside the text itself. Several essays were solicited from eminent African scholars who, having taught abroad, know firsthand the challenges of conveying cross-cultural understanding through African literature. Chinua Achebe graciously agreed to make a brief introductory statement, even though he claims never to have formally taught *Things Fall Apart* in a classroom, having held firm to the principle that under certain circumstances novelists ought not to be teachers, at least not of their own novels.

The volume is divided into two sections. The first, entitled "Materials," offers descriptions of available editions, reference works, secondary sources, and aids to teaching. It was compiled from the responses to a questionnaire sent to several hundred African literature teachers throughout North America and parts of Africa and Europe. The survey provides a record of the methods and materials used to teach Achebe's novel. To this body of data I have added references to significant studies of Achebe published since the survey was made.

The second section, "Approaches," contains Achebe's statement and sixteen essays by a cross section of instructors who were invited to describe in detail one aspect of their approaches to teaching the novel. The volume concludes with a list of those who participated in the survey, a bibliography of works cited, and an index of proper names.

I hope this book proves useful to teachers in many instructional situations. Its pedagogical approaches to the best-known work by Africa's best-known novelist not only provide teachers with models to emulate but also serve to stimulate and encourage them as they introduce their students to a classic text from another culture.

Educators who elect to teach such works enhance their students' understanding of the world and its peoples. They also help open up the traditional English studies canon, a worthy goal in itself, by transporting students to a fresh imaginative terrain that illustrates the remarkable literary consequences of the internationalization of the English language. Through this experience, readers in different corners of the globe become conscious of belonging to a single, multinational language community. Suddenly they find a whole new universe of thought and feeling available to them in their own language, a universe that puts them in intimate touch with people in other parts of the world. Readers everywhere may enter Achebe's Igbo worldview and see past and present African experiences from an indigenous perspective. Teaching *Things Fall Apart* thus serves to draw different peoples closer together.

BL

Part One

MATERIALS

Editions

Three paperback editions of *Things Fall Apart* are in print in the United States—one published by Heinemann Educational Books in its African Writers Series, another by Fawcett Crest, and a third by Astor-Honor—but only the Heinemann edition is sold elsewhere. Teachers in North America tend to prefer the Heinemann edition because it is readily available, attractively designed, and usefully supplemented with a brief biographical note on the author, a glossary of Igbo words and phrases, and the lines in W. B. Yeats's "Second Coming" from which the novel takes its title. Those who prefer the Fawcett Crest edition note that it is easy to order in large quantities and that it contains the same glossary that the Heinemann edition features. Few use the Astor-Honor edition. Some teachers who responded to the survey express no strong preference for a particular edition, saying that availability is more important to them than price or design. Since the Heinemann edition is the most popular one in the United States and since no other edition is distributed internationally, all page citations in this volume are from the 1988 reprint of Heinemann's African Writers Series text. The Heinemann edition has sold over three million copies throughout the world.

Reference Works

Bibliographies

The most recent bibliography devoted exclusively to Achebe and his works was compiled by Cele Uwechie, Moses Ugwoke, and the staff at the University of Nigeria, Nsukka, and published in 1990. It contains 1,453 entries; of these, 287 are works by Achebe (novels, children's literature, nonfiction, poetry, short stories, translations) and 1,166 are works about Achebe (bibliographies, biographies, interviews, book reviews, literary criticism, theses, dissertations). A less comprehensive listing by B. Okpu, published as a seventy-page pamphlet in Nigeria in 1984, has 759 entries: 154 primary texts and 605 secondary sources. Unfortunately, neither bibliography is marketed outside Nigeria, so teachers elsewhere may have to turn to earlier compilations, such as the bibliography in *Achebe's World: The Historical and Cultural Context of the Novels of Chinua Achebe*, by Robert M. Wren; the three volumes of *Black African Literature in English*, by Bernth Lindfors; or the bibliography appended to *Chinua Achebe*, a new critical study by C. L. Innes. For leads to the latest articles and books on Achebe, teachers may consult the annual African literature bibliographies in the *MLA International Bibliography*, the *Journal of Commonwealth Literature*, and *Callaloo*.

Biographical Sources and Interviews

Biographical information on Achebe can be found in Janheinz Jahn, Ulla Schild, and Almut Nordmann's *Who's Who in African Literature*; Donald E. Herdeck's *African Authors: A Companion to Black African Writing*; Hans M. Zell, Carol Bundy, and Virginia Coulon's *New Reader's Guide to African Literature*; James A. Page and Jae Min Roh's *Selected Black American, African, and Caribbean Authors: A Bio-Bibliography*; and Ada Ugah's *In the Beginning . . . : Chinua Achebe at Work*, as well as in Achebe's charming autobiographical essay "Named for Victoria, Queen of England." One may also glean interesting biographical information from interviews with Achebe, particularly those collected in *African Writers Talking: A Collection of Radio Interviews*, edited by Dennis Duerden and Cosmo Pieterse; *Palaver: Interviews with Five African Writers in Texas*, edited by Bernth Lindfors, Ian Munro, Richard Priebe, and Reinhard Sander; *In Person: Achebe, Awoonor, and Soyinka at the University of Washington*, edited by Karen L. Morell; and *Towards African Literary Independence: A Dialogue with Contemporary African Writers*, edited by Phanuel Akubueze Egejuru. "Chinua Achebe: At the Crossroads," an interview by Jonathan Cott, and "Chinua Achebe: Nigerian Novelist," an interview by Bill Moyers, provide useful information as well. Interviews by Ernest Emenyonu and Pat Emenyonu in *Africa Report*, Chinweizu in *Okike*, Kalu Ogbaa in *Research in African Literatures*, Michael Awoyinfa in *Sunday Concord Magazine*, and Okey Ndibe and C. Don Adinuba in *African Guardian* shed valuable light not only on *Things Fall Apart* but also on Achebe's later writings. A list of published interviews with Achebe in books, journals, magazines, and newspapers appears in each volume of Lindfors's *Black African Literature in English*.

Igbo Studies

For background information on the Igbo (Ibo) people, the handiest single bibliographical source is Joseph C. Anafulu's *Ibo-Speaking Peoples of Southern Nigeria: A Selected Annotated List of Writings, 1627–1970*, which supersedes useful earlier bibliographical efforts by Anafulu ("Igbo Life"), Simon Ottenberg, and C. D. Forde and G. I. Jones. More general reference works concerned with Nigeria as a whole are Christian Chukwunedu Aguolu's *Nigeria: A Comprehensive Bibliography in the Humanities and Social Sciences, 1900–1971* and Nduntuei O. Ita's *Bibliography of Nigeria: A Sur-*

vey of Anthropological and Linguistic Writings from the Earliest Times to 1966; Ita's work has a separate section dealing with the Igbo people. Teachers can encourage graduate students and advanced undergraduates to consult these sources independently for leads to relevant scholarship, but freshmen and sophomores may need guidance to the most useful studies of Igbo life and history.

Readings for Students and Teachers

Background Studies: Anthropology, History, Politics, Religion

Some teachers, as one survey respondent writes, like to "keep students focused on a text and let the background come out of the text, as it were," while others seek to immerse students in supplementary readings that relate the story told in *Things Fall Apart* to African colonial experience in general and to the harsh historical experience of the Igbo people in particular. Among North American teachers the favorite background book on the Igbo is Victor C. Uchendu's *Igbo of Southeast Nigeria*, a brief anthropological monograph containing useful chapters on government, kinship, hospitality, status placement, and religious beliefs. Uchendu, an Igbo, speaks with the authority of an insider, someone who has grown up in the culture he describes. The next most frequently recommended background text is Robert M. Wren's *Achebe's World*, a richly detailed account of the historical and cultural context of Achebe's first four novels that gives due attention to the transformation of traditional Igbo society under the pressure of British colonial authority. Wren also offers a helpful note on pidgin English; an informative glossary of key names, places, and terms; and a valuable selected bibliography of historical and anthropological sources on the Igbo people. This book, possibly more than any other, enables readers to place the drama enacted in *Things Fall Apart* in its proper physical and temporal setting. Teachers who assign or encourage background reading ought to ensure that Uchendu's and Wren's books are available to students.

For teachers and students who wish to delve even further into Igbo life and history, many additional books can be recommended. Among the most important for Achebe studies are anthropological classics such as G. T. Basden's *Niger Ibos*, M. M. Green's *Ibo Village Affairs*, C. D. Forde and G. I. Jones's *Ibo and Ibibio-Speaking Peoples of South-eastern Nigeria*, Percy Amaury Talbot's *In the Shadow of the Bush*, Northcote W. Thomas's *Anthropological Report on the Ibo-Speaking Peoples of Nigeria*, and A. G. Leonard's *Lower Niger and Its Tribes*. Major historical studies include K. Onwuka Dike's *Trade and Politics in the Niger Delta, 1830–1835: An Intro-*

duction to the Economic and Political History of Nigeria, J. C. Anene's *Southern Nigeria in Transition, 1885–1906: Theory and Practice in a Colonial Protectorate*, Elizabeth Isichei's *History of the Igbo People* and *Ibo People and the Europeans: The Genesis of a Relationship—to 1906*, A. E. Afigbo's *Warrant Chiefs: Indirect Rule in Southeastern Nigeria, 1891–1929* and *Ropes of Sand: Studies in Igbo History and Culture*, E. A. Ayandele's *Missionary Impact on Modern Nigeria, 1842–1914: A Political and Social Analysis*, Mazi E. N. Njaka's *Igbo Political Culture*, and Thurstan Shaw's *Unearthing Igbo-Ukwu: Archaeological Discoveries in Eastern Nigeria*. The bibliography in Wren's *Achebe's World* lists additional relevant titles.

Some teachers who use *Things Fall Apart* in introductory courses on African history prefer to pair the novel with a text such as Basil Davidson's *History of West Africa to the Nineteenth Century*, Roland Oliver and J. D. Fage's *Short History of Africa*, or Michael Crowder's *Short History of Nigeria* so that students see the African colonial experience in a broader historical perspective. Others who teach the novel as part of a course on Third World literature or politics or both recommend using it in conjunction with books such as Walter Rodney's *How Europe Underdeveloped Africa*, Frantz Fanon's *Wretched of the Earth* and *Dying Colonialism*, Amilcar Cabral's *Return to the Source*, Peter Worsley's *Three Worlds: Culture and World Development*, and Chancellor Williams's *Destruction of Black Civilization*. These books, one survey participant comments, "introduce the sociohistorical parameters of colonialism and the spectrum of cultural and political responses available in the context of colonialism." Teachers who select *Things Fall Apart* for courses principally concerned with culture, religion, or philosophy find it profitable to have students read the novel alongside broad introductory surveys such as Paul Bohannan and Philip Curtin's *Africa and Africans*, Eric O. Ayisi's *Introduction to the Study of African Culture*, Elechi Amadi's *Ethics in Nigerian Culture*, Adrian Hastings's *African Christianity*, John Mbiti's *Introduction to African Religion* and *African Religions and Philosophy*, W. E. Abraham's *Mind of Africa*, and Claude Wauthier's *Literature and Thought of Modern Africa*. For elucidation of a key Igbo philosophical concept in the novel, many experienced teachers turn to Achebe's essay "Chi in Igbo Cosmology."

Critical Commentary

The distinguished Igbo historian Elizabeth Isichei once remarked, in a review of Wren's *Achebe's World*, "Critical writing on Chinua Achebe is an academic growth industry, and probably more has been written about him than about any single aspect of Igbo history or culture" (414). Twelve critical books on Achebe and his works have already appeared: G. D. Killam's *Novels of Chinua Achebe*, David Carroll's *Chinua Achebe*, Thomas Melone's *Chinua*

Achebe et la tragédie de l'histoire, Arthur Ravenscroft's *Chinua Achebe*, Robert M. Wren's *Achebe's World*, Benedict Chiaka Njoku's *Four Novels of Chinua Achebe: A Critical Study*, Denise Coussy's *L'oeuvre de Chinua Achebe*, Emmanuel Meziemadu Okoye's *Traditional Religion and Its Encounter with Christianity in Achebe's Novels*, Kalu Ogbaa's *Folkways in Chinua Achebe's Novels*, Prospero Trigona's *La maledizione del serpente: Saggio sulla narrativa di Chinua Achebe*, Kofi E. Yankson's *Chinua Achebe's Novels: A Sociolinguistic Perspective*, and C. L. Innes's *Chinua Achebe*. Teachers frequently recommend the books by Killam, Carroll, and Wren to their students, and many will probably add Innes's new book to their select list of supplementary readings as soon as this study becomes more well known. The works by Melone and Njoku are flawed by factual errors, and the more specialized recent studies by Okoye, Ogbaa, and Yankson, though useful for insights into Achebe's handling of religion, folklore, and language, are not as widely available in North American libraries as the others are. The works by Ravenscroft and Coussy offer brief but illuminating comments on *Things Fall Apart*. Teachers seeking to expose their students to a variety of critical views sometimes assign selections from *Critical Perspectives on Chinua Achebe*, edited by C. L. Innes and Bernth Lindfors, which contains twenty-two essays, half of them concerned with *Things Fall Apart*.

Achebe is featured in nearly every critical book on modern African literature. Among the works survey participants recommend for students and teachers are a dozen broad introductory surveys: Kofi Awoonor's *Breast of the Earth: A Survey of the History, Culture, and Literature of Africa South of the Sahara*, Wilfred Cartey's *Whispers from a Continent: Writings from Contemporary Black Africa*, David Cook's *African Literature: A Critical View*, Abiola Irele's *African Experience in Literature and Ideology*, Janheinz Jahn's *History of Neo-African Literature: Writing in Two Continents*, Gerald Moore's *Twelve African Writers*, Ezekiel Mphahlele's *African Image*, James Olney's *Tell Me Africa: An Approach to African Literature*, Oyekan Owomoyela's *African Literatures: An Introduction*, Adrian Roscoe's *Mother Is Gold*, Oladele Taiwo's *Introduction to West African Literature*, and Martin Tucker's *Africa in Modern Literature*. The most frequently cited critical works dealing specifically with fiction are Simon Gikandi's *Reading the African Novel*, Judith Gleason's *This Africa: Novels by West Africans in English and French*, Charles R. Larson's *Emergence of African Fiction*, Margaret Laurence's *Long Drums and Cannons: Nigerian Dramatists and Novelists, 1952–1966*, Neil McEwen's *Africa and the Novel*, Eustace Palmer's *Introduction to the African Novel* and *Growth of the African Novel*, and Oladele Taiwo's *Culture and the Nigerian Novel*. Some teachers comment favorably on innovative comparative studies such as Micere Githae-Mugo's *Visions of Africa: The Fiction of Chinua Achebe, Margaret Laurence, Elspeth Huxley, and Ngugi wa Thiong'o*, Gareth Griffeths's *Double Exile: African and West*

Indian Writing between Two Cultures, Abdul R. JanMohamed's *Manichean Aesthetics: The Politics of Literature in Colonial Africa*, and Jonathan Peters's *Dance of Masks: Senghor, Achebe, Soyinka*. Other teachers recommend books examining the effect of African tradition on modern literary creativity, especially titles such as Janheinz Jahn's *Muntu: An Outline of the New African Culture*, Bernth Lindfors's *Folklore in Nigerian Literature*, Emmanuel Obiechina's *Culture, Tradition, and Society in the West African Novel*, Richard K. Priebe's *Myth, Realism, and the West African Writer*, and Wole Soyinka's *Myth, Literature, and the African World*. Teachers may add to this list James Booth's *Writers and Politics in Nigeria*, Ernest Emenyonu's *Rise of the Igbo Novel*, and Lindfors's *Early Nigerian Literature*, books attempting to contextualize Achebe's achievement by setting it in an appropriate ethnic or national literary milieu. One source that several respondents find helpful pedagogically is Elizabeth Gunner's *Handbook for Teaching African Literature*, which includes a short chapter offering practical suggestions for teachers of *Things Fall Apart*.

More than two dozen study guides have been published on *Things Fall Apart*, most of them intended for high school examination candidates in Africa. Most of these guides have little critical significance, but a few make a modest contribution to a better understanding of the novel. Recommended guides include those by David Attwell, Christopher Heywood (*Critical View*), Kate Turkington, and Robert M. Wren (*Chinua Achebe*).

Achebe has been the subject of hundreds of critical essays, many of which deal with *Things Fall Apart*. Among the most memorable of these brief critiques are studies of language and style by Gareth Griffeths ("Language and Action"), C. L. Innes ("Language"), Eldred Jones, Emmanuel Obiechina ("Problem"), Austin J. Shelton, Theo Vincent, and Marjorie Winters ("Objective Approach"); explorations of narrative technique by Romanus N. Egudu, Solomon O. Iyasere, Abdul R. JanMohamed ("Sophisticated"), and Clement A. Okafor; explications of imagery and symbolism by Christopher Heywood ("Surface and Symbol"), Bu-Buakei Jabbi, Russell McDougall, Emmanuel Obiechina ("Structure and Significance"), Donald Weinstock, and Donald Weinstock and Cathy Ramadan; investigations of characterization by Oyekan Owomoyela ("Chinua Achebe"), Eustace Palmer ("Character"), and Harold Scheub; observations on elements of tragedy in the novel by Robert Fraser, Abiola Irele ("Tragic Conflict"), Kalu Ogbaa ("Cultural Note"), and Richard K. Priebe ("Fate"); and accounts of Achebe's critical reception by Ebele Eko, Raoul Granqvist ("Early Swedish"; "Achebe's Language"), J. Z. Kronenfeld, and Marjorie Winters ("Morning").

Achebe's artistry has been compared with that of many other writers. Teachers who encourage their students to draw such comparisons might recommend essays by Cecil A. Abrahams, Yédiéti Edouard Coulibaly, Ernest

Emenyonu ("Early Fiction"), H. H. Anniah Gowda, Steven Jervis, E. V. Ramkrishnan, A. G. Stock, Bernard Timberg, Nelson Wattie, Philip G. Williams, and Sylvia Wynter, who compare *Things Fall Apart* to works by such diverse authors as Ahmed Ali, James Baldwin, Ralph Ellison, Gabriel García Márquez, Thomas Hardy, Witi Ihimaera, George Lamming, Margaret Laurence, Camara Laye, Peter Nwana, Chaim Potok, and W. B. Yeats. Another ploy is to have students contrast *Things Fall Apart* with a Western novel about Africa, such as Joseph Conrad's *Heart of Darkness* or Joyce Cary's *Mister Johnson* (the novel that prompted Achebe to begin writing long fiction). Those who adopt this approach would be well advised to consult "An Image of Africa," Achebe's essay on *Heart of Darkness* in *Hopes and Impediments*, as well as the controversy that followed in responses by Patrick Brantlinger, Wilson Harris, Hunt Hawkins, Reinhardt Kuesgen, P. J. M. Robertson, C. P. Sarvan, Cedric Watts, and Henryk Zins. For comparisons of Achebe and Cary, one may turn to Wren's *Achebe's World* and an essay by Brian W. Last, as well as to Achebe's own remarks in an interview with Lewis Nkosi published in *African Writers Talking* (ed. Duerden and Pieterse).

Some teachers assign more than one Achebe novel in a single course, linking *Things Fall Apart* with a story of more modern times—usually its sequel, *No Longer at Ease*, which focuses on a later generation in the same family, or *A Man of the People*. Several teachers use *Things Fall Apart* as a warm-up exercise for *Arrow of God*, Achebe's most ambitious work set in a traditional Igbo society, and a few juxtapose his earliest novel with *Anthills of the Savannah* (1987), which deals with military rule in postcolonial Africa. Because Achebe's works are thematically related and therefore lend themselves to comparison with one another, they often serve as the best foil to *Things Fall Apart*.

Instructors frequently require that students read a selection of Achebe's critical essays, most of which are collected in *Morning Yet on Creation Day* and *Hopes and Impediments*. Teachers most commonly assign "The African Writer and the English Language," which appears in *Morning*, and "The Novelist as Teacher," which is reprinted in both volumes. Another of his famous critical statements, "The Role of the Writer in a New Nation," which presents a rationale for writing realistic historical fiction, can be found in *African Writers on African Writing*, edited by G. D. Killam. In "The Black Writer's Burden" and "The African Writer and the Biafran Cause," Achebe argues that African authors ought to turn their attention to contemporary problems. Students may also enjoy reading *The Trouble with Nigeria*, his controlled diatribe on Nigerian political leadership. All these polemical pieces offer evidence of Achebe's acuity and persuasiveness as a critic as well as of his superb artistry as an essayist. Some of his finest writing appears in essay form.

Audiovisual Aids

The Story

Three films have been based on *Things Fall Apart*. The earliest and least successful was made in Nigeria in the early 1970s as a joint Nigram-Calpenny-Cine 3 production. Originally called *Bullfrog in the Sun* and later renamed *Things Fall Apart*, it attempts to combine the story of Okonkwo with that of his grandson Obi, the protagonist of Achebe's second novel, *No Longer at Ease*; the results are less than satisfactory. The film was screened commercially in parts of tropical Africa but was not seen widely in the United States, though it still turns up occasionally as a late-night selection on American cable television channels. For a fuller description of it, see Charles R. Larson's "Film Version of *Things Fall Apart*."

In the mid-1980s, the Nigerian Television Authority made an elaborate new film version that is more faithful to the novel. First shown on Nigerian television in 1986, this dramatic interpretation of *Things Fall Apart* is now available in the United States on videocassette. However, teachers wishing to use this film in the classroom should be warned that it is an epic production, consisting of thirteen hour-long episodes. Instructors may wish to select a key episode or two for screening. For leads to reviews of it in the Nigerian press, see Nancy Schmidt's *Sub-Saharan African Films and Filmmakers: An Annotated Bibliography*.

A third dramatized version, produced for television broadcast in eastern Nigeria, was filmed entirely in the Igbo language. This film is not available outside Nigeria.

The Author

At least three filmed interviews with Achebe are available. In the earliest, the fourth in the African Writers of Today series filmed by the Transcription Centre in 1964, he is interviewed by Lewis Nkosi and Wole Soyinka. This film can be rented from the Audio-Visual Center at Indiana University (Bloomington, IN 47401). The Archives of Traditional Music at Indiana University has an audio recording of the same interview, a partial transcript of which was published in *African Writers Talking* (ed. Duerden and Pieterse) and in *Africa Report* (Nkosi).

In 1986, Nuruddin Farah interviewed Achebe at the Institute of Contemporary Arts in London. Videocassettes of this interview can be obtained from the ICA (Nash House, The Mall, London SW1Y 5AH). For reactions to the interview, see the reports by Herbert Ekwe-Ekwe, Patricia Morris, and Karen Woolfson.

In 1988, shortly after publication of his *Anthills of the Savannah* in the United States, Achebe was interviewed by Bill Moyers on "A World of Ideas," a television show on the Public Broadcasting Service. A videotape of the interview can be obtained from PBS Video (1320 Braddock Place, Alexandria, VA 22314; 800 424-7963). An edited transcript of the interview has been published in Moyers's *World of Ideas*.

The Language Lab at the University of Texas, Austin (Austin, TX 78712), has videotapes of Achebe giving a public lecture, "The Writer and His Community," in the spring of 1988 (the full text was later published as an essay in *Hopes and Impediments*) and answering questions from students in an African literature class. Similar videotapes may be available at other campuses where Achebe has spoken or taught.

The American Audio Prose Library, Inc. (P.O. Box 842, Columbus, MO 65205), has released two ninety-minute audiocassettes, one an interview with Achebe covering his entire writing career, the other a recording of his reading of excerpts from *Arrow of God* and *Anthills of the Savannah*.

Part Two

APPROACHES

INTRODUCTION

When asked to explain why they teach *Things Fall Apart*, survey respondents had several basic answers. One teacher, echoing the comments of many, strives to "give students a sense of African history and the effects of colonialism on Africa, as well as to dispel stereotypes about Africa." Others say they also want students "to come to grips with the whole question of Africa's relation to the Western world" and "to examine the very complicated process of internal contradictions and external invasions" portrayed by Achebe. *Things Fall Apart*, another respondent notes, "offers an unusual opportunity to discover the foreign from within," thereby encouraging students to develop a less parochial outlook on the world. Further, this novel depicts a "significant historical moment in Third World experience"; it is "a major literary anti-imperialist statement."

But most English teachers select *Things Fall Apart* primarily for its aesthetic qualities: they describe it variously as "first-rate literature," "an example of clear, concise, and evocative writing," a book "deceptively simple linguistically, structurally, and thematically and thus pedagogically stimulating and challenging to analyze." Indeed, respondents call Achebe's work "*the* classic," "the most read book of its time," and "a key African literary text" that helps to "win students away from a Eurocentric notion of canon." One teacher recommends the book "for its art, its humanity, its honesty—primarily, its story." Others comment that *Things Fall Apart* provides "perhaps the best introduction to postcolonial English literature" and that "it is accessible to students who rarely read." Because the book is "so readable and well made, it is ideal for an introduction to literature." With these credentials, *Things Fall Apart* surely will remain one of the most widely taught literary classics from the Third World for many generations to come.

Instructors will also continue to teach the novel in a variety of ways. In the essays that follow Chinua Achebe's introductory statement, sixteen experienced instructors describe how they choose to teach *Things Fall Apart.* Each essay concentrates on a single strategy for introducing students to the novel and its author. As might be expected, instructional tactics vary considerably and depend on the context in which the book is taught. Some teachers use it as a core text in survey courses on black, African, or Third World literatures; others include it in courses on the novel, often setting it in opposition to representative works from the literature of empire; still others teach it primarily as an excellent example of evocative prose fiction. The responses to the survey of university instructors in North America and abroad reveal that *Things Fall Apart* has become required reading in many different courses, ranging from advanced graduate seminars on fiction, criticism, and literary theory to basic undergraduate staples such as introductory literature and humanities courses and even freshman composition.

The seventeen essays are grouped into seven sections; the first three essays provide background information on the author and the world represented in his novel. Chinua Achebe's introductory essay comments on reactions *Things Fall Apart* has elicited from readers around the world and addresses several frequently asked questions about the fate of his hero. Although Achebe claims to be no expert in teaching his own work, he offers useful advice on probing the deep structure of his narrative and discovering the significance of his story. The essays by Simon Gikandi and Emmanuel Obiechina then suggest ways of approaching the novel through an examination of the attitudes, opinions, and cultural orientation of the author. Gikandi presents relevant biographical information on Achebe, summarizing positions the author has expressed in interviews and autobiographical essays, studying novels Achebe read before starting to write fiction, and then looking for evidence of the imprint of his experience on the style, structure, and ideology of *Things Fall Apart.* But Gikandi also encourages students to resist interpretations of the novel that are too narrowly focused on the background and ideas of the author; readers should respond to the text on its own terms, looking for its deep structure rather than its obedience to the author's stated intentions. Obiechina's essay, however, proceeds inductively, searching the text for the verbal signposts through which Achebe conveys his insights and ideas. Achebe, Obiechina maintains, is so skillful a teacher that no attentive reader is likely to mistake his meaning. Close textual study is all the student needs to understand the author and the world of experience contained in his art.

In the next section, Robert M. Wren and Dan Izevbaye provide the kind of historical and ethnological background information that many teachers requested in the survey questionnaire. Wren identifies actual historical events that are sometimes directly and other times obliquely reflected in *Things*

Fall Apart. He also locates specific colonial, anthropological, and historical texts that may have had a formative influence on Achebe's depiction of traditional Igbo society. Izevbaye treats colonial history too, but he emphasizes the ways the Igbo differed from other ethnic groups in Nigeria and how these differences in custom and culture made the colonial government more difficult for the British to administer. Though the novel depicts an abnormal historical situation involving exceptional colonial subjects, Achebe's powerful reinterpretation of the African past has already gained the stature of an archetypal historical myth.

The volume's next two contributions focus on aspects of the novel's texture. Ashton Nichols discusses the advantages of teaching *Things Fall Apart* from the perspective of shifting and multiple points of view; such an approach ultimately encourages students to interrogate their assumptions about cultures and about literature. Arlene A. Elder examines in detail Achebe's characterization of Okonkwo, finding it a paradoxical portrait of a protagonist who is both a typical Igbo man and an individualist; students made aware of these contradictory qualities may be able to recognize in Okonkwo the suicidal fragmentation of Igbo society during the colonial era. Both pedagogical approaches emphasize Achebe's artistry in creating a complex and convincing fictional world.

The next section deals with comparative approaches to *Things Fall Apart.* First, Ousseynou B. Traoré and Barbara Harlow investigate Achebe's adroit use of traditional oral narrative paradigms to communicate cultural and political ideas. Traoré employs a matrical approach to study the narrative grammar of the novel and thereby to explore important formal and thematic issues. Harlow, restricting her focus to a single fable inserted in the novel, argues that this tale functions within the larger narrative as an allegory of resistance, with the greedy tortoise representing colonial power and the exploited birds standing for the oppressed colonized population. Traditional lore is thus pressed into service to carry a pertinent political message about Africa's colonial history.

Two other comparative approaches to the novel stress its intertextuality with modern literary works. Hunt Hawkins finds it fruitful to teach *Things Fall Apart* alongside novels of empire by Joseph Conrad, Rudyard Kipling, E. M. Forster, George Orwell, Joyce Cary, and Graham Greene, for the stance taken by Achebe serves as a necessary corrective to the proimperialist bias of the British authors. Edna Aizenberg compares *Things Fall Apart* with *Men of Maize* by the Guatemalan author Miguel Angel Asturias to demonstrate that both works can be read as fictional counterhistories that reconstruct the past from the point of view of the vanquished. Because Achebe's novel shares a commonality of spirit with great works of Latin American historical fiction, it speaks not only for Africa but also for other parts of the Third World.

The next four essays develop approaches that challenge conventional notions of *Things Fall Apart*. In a deconstructive feminist critique, Rhonda Cobham scrutinizes Achebe's selective presentation of Igbo and Christian values and discovers that this kind of selectivity in the evocation of a traditional African social reality results in an inadequate rendering of the role of women in Igbo society. Achebe affirms traditional and Judeo-Christian patriarchal values simultaneously, thereby suppressing the record of women's contributions to the Igbo past. Cobham feels that Achebe's overly masculine interpretation of African colonial history needs to be challenged and revised by today's African women writers. Zohreh T. Sullivan, following a different line of argument, uses Bakhtin's notion of multivoiced discourse to explore dialogic aspects of Achebe's art. She also attempts to situate the novel historically and politically in order to study Achebe's conflictive relation to the world he seeks to re-create in fiction. In the classroom Sullivan highlights the paradoxes and problems inherent in such fiction so that students can gain a fuller understanding of the disturbing instabilities of decolonized discourse. Wahneema Lubiano's essay also demonstrates the narrative complexity of *Things Fall Apart* but focuses primarily on Achebe's adroit handling of language, metacommentary, and a nonlinear plot line. She maintains that this novel is not the simple anthropological tale that Eurocentric readers have assumed it to be but rather a highly sophisticated literary text with postmodern properties that advance and invigorate its political argument. The job of the teacher is to bring out these unperceived qualities, to recover the "repressed" form of the text. Finally, Biodun Jeyifo, in a Marxist exegesis, sees *Things Fall Apart* as a canonical Third World text that appeals to readers everywhere because its seemingly objective realism renders with poignancy and solicitude the plight of the powerless and the dominated. But this realism has an inner logic, an internal dialectic that emerges most clearly in the initial encounter between colonizer and colonized and its tragically destructive aftermath, when new oppressions and alienations begin to surface. In other words, despite his striving to remain dispassionately neutral, Achebe cannot wholly avoid inserting an ideological bias into his interpretation of the historical past. Again, the teacher should make an effort to sensitize students to such submerged but significant countercurrents in the text.

After these provocative interpretations come two essays outlining approaches to teaching *Things Fall Apart* in special curricular contexts. Eric Sellin describes a method of including the novel in an undergraduate humanities core course, and Richard K. Priebe tells how he incorporates it in a practical criticism course. These two essays identify only a few of the available options, for the novel fits comfortably into many other niches in the curriculum. As mentioned earlier, *Things Fall Apart* has been frequently used in courses in history, politics, anthropology, folklore, ethnic studies, and African studies. Teachers report that it is a popular text among students and a pleasure to teach. In the years to come, as it is adopted in more and more instructional contexts, new approaches to teaching *Things Fall Apart* are bound to emerge.

THE AUTHOR AS TEACHER

Teaching *Things Fall Apart*

Chinua Achebe

I can see a number of reasons why I should be asked to contribute to a book on the teaching of *Things Fall Apart*. The first and most obvious is, of course, that I wrote the book. As obvious reasons go, this is perhaps not such a bad one. I have known the book if not more intimately, then at least for a longer period than anybody else around. And a teacher's coming to ask me about it is rather like a journalist's ferreting out the mother of a young man who has suddenly shot into fame or, more likely, infamy.

A second reason might be that I have taught literature in African and American universities for almost twenty years and should have learned a thing or two that I could pass on. That too is a good reason. But there might even be a third and problematic one, namely, that I once gave a paper at a conference in Leeds, England, which I titled rather unwisely "The Novelist as Teacher"; as a consequence everything pertaining to classrooms has been referred to me ever since! And I have kept muttering, "That is not what I meant at all. That is not it, at all!" To no effect whatsoever.

Now let's go back for a moment to the mother of the man in the news. Her attitude, if she has sufficient toughness, ought to be, "When I gave birth to him I fulfilled all my obligations to you. Now get out!" The Igbo wrap it more politely in a nice proverb and place it in the mouth of mother-monkey. She says, "I can speak for the little one inside my belly; as for the little one on my back, ask him yourself."

There is a further complication. Because I wrote *Things Fall Apart* I have never taught it. Although I have never felt particularly disadvantaged on that score, I now realize that I cannot bring to this essay actual, concrete classroom experience as I might do if the book in question were, shall we say, *The Palm-Wine Drinkard* or *July's People*.

But my disadvantage is not, I hope, entirely crippling. For I do have other kinds of experience garnered from diverse encounters with readers and critics, students and teachers in the past thirty years. I have even, on occasions such as public lectures, attempted to reflect on some of the opinions expressed in these encounters.

Letters are, of course, quite special in my view, for when a reader has been sufficiently moved (or even perturbed) by a book to sit down and compose a letter to the author, something very powerful has happened. *Things Fall Apart* has brought me a large body of such correspondence from people of different ages and backgrounds all over the world.

These letters have generally come singly and at leisurely intervals. But a few months ago I received a bulky manila envelope that turned out to contain thirty-odd letters from a whole English honors class in a woman's college in South Korea! The students had just read *Things Fall Apart* and had been moved to write me individually. Although I knew that the book had been making remarkable inroads into the Far East in recent years, I was not quite prepared for such a bumper response as the Korean letters. I frame my present thoughts around some of the issues in these letters.

But let me first make one general point that is fundamental and essential to the appreciation of African issues by Americans. Africans are people in the same way that Americans, Europeans, Asians, and others are people. Africans are not some strange beings with unpronounceable names and impenetrable minds. Although the action of *Things Fall Apart* takes place in a setting with which most Americans are unfamiliar, the characters are normal people and their events are real human events. The necessity even to say this is part of a burden imposed on us by the customary denigration of Africa in the popular imagination of the West. I suspect that, in any class of thirty American students who are reading *Things Fall Apart*, there are a handful who see things in the light of a certain young reader from Yonkers, New York, who wrote to thank me several years ago for making available to him an account of the customs and superstitions of an African tribe! It should be the pleasant task of the teacher, should he or she encounter that attitude, to spend a little time revealing to the class some of the quaint customs and superstitions prevalent in America.

Fortunately, not everyone in that class would be a hidebound ethnocentrist. Indeed I hope that at least one person would resemble not the Yonkers student or worse but another young man who, having read *Things Fall Apart* in a course, came up to me while I was visiting the University of Massachusetts. He wore a very intense look, and all he wanted to say was, "That Okonkwo is like my father." And he was a white kid.

Now the extraordinary thing about this incident is that a few years later I heard the very same testimony again, except that this time it came from a very distinguished black American—James Baldwin. He was responding to a question put to him at the African Literature Association Conference in Gainesville, Florida, in 1980:

> When I read *Things Fall Apart* in Paris . . . [about] the Ibo tribe in Nigeria . . . a tribe I never saw; a system, to put it that way, or a society the rules of which were a mystery to me . . . I recognized everybody in it. That book was about my father. . . . How he got over I don't know but he did.

No one can suggest that every reader or indeed that many readers of *Things Fall Apart* should come up with similar recognitions. That would make Okonkwo a typical human being, which he certainly is not; he is not even a typical Igbo. But this incident does suggest that, in spite of serious cultural differences, it is possible for readers in the West to identify, even deeply, with characters and situations in an African novel.

The young women from Korea responded to a wide range of topics in the book; I mention only a few key issues here that, in a way, are also representative of responses that have come to me from other quarters over the years. But the letters brought something new as well—that Korean readers draw a parallel between the colonization of the Igbo people by the British in the nineteenth century and that of their own country by Japan in the twentieth. I must say that the depth of bitterness I glimpsed from several of these letters concerning colonization was more profound than anything one encounters in Africa today. And the book must have unlocked for these young readers the door to Okonkwo's suffering mind and brought close a tragedy that happened far away and long ago. From that shared community of pain, some of them wanted to know why, in their words, I let Okonkwo fail.

I have been asked this question in one form or another by a certain kind of reader for thirty years: Why did you allow a just cause to stumble and fall? The best I can do for an answer is to say that it is in the nature of things. This response leads me directly into the carefully laid ambush of the doctrinaire statement, "Well, we knew you would say that. But it is not enough for us that our art should merely report the nature of things; it should aim to change it."

I agree, of course, about good art changing things. But art doesn't go about promoting change in the uncomplicated, linear equivalency of sympathetic magic, which would send its practitioner scouring the forest for spotted leaves to cure a patient who has broken out in spots. That is not medicine but charlatanism.

Good causes can and do fail even when the people who espouse and lead them are not themselves in one way or another severely flawed. This theme is of course the stuff of tragedy in literature and is well-known. But the concepts of success and failure as commonly used in this connection are inadequate. Did Okonkwo fail? In a certain sense, he did, obviously. But he also left behind a story strong enough to make those who hear it even in faraway Korea wish devoutly that things had gone differently for him.

More than one Korean student took issue with me over the manner of Okonkwo's dying. Again, this subject has come up before in discussions and in criticism. I don't know what Korean traditional culture teaches about suicide. Western culture, we know, views it as moral cowardice or simply as copping out, thus trivializing it into a matter between an individual and his or her problems. In Okonkwo's world suicide is a monumental issue between an individual, on the one hand, and, on the other, society and all its divinities including titulary gods and ancestors—indeed the entire cosmos. People who commit suicide put themselves beyond every conceivable pale.

Okonkwo is a rash man, and it is unlikely that he has reasoned out the final moments and actions of his life. But even he must also exemplify the Igbo saying: "The thought that leads a man to kill himself cannot be merely one night old." Events have been urging him toward total rupture with his world. Finally, when this world crumbles so miserably and so disgracefully under attack, Okonkwo, who has never learned to live with failure, separates himself from it with ultimate, eschatological defiance.

While on the subject of last things, I might as well bring up in conclusion the question of the very last words of the novel, which, as I recall, used to embroil critics in considerable argument. The distinguished American scholar and teacher Jules Chametzky opens his book *Our Decentralized Literature* with a discussion of that aspect of the novel. Since his point agrees well with what I might call the narrative intention of the story's ending, I shall save my breath and quote somewhat lengthily from it:

> In the last paragraph of Chinua Achebe's *Things Fall Apart*—perhaps the most memorable account in English of an African culture and the impact upon it of white European encroachment—the voice and language of the book shifts with startling abruptness. . . . Anyone who has read or taught this novel can testify to the outrageous reductionism of this last paragraph, especially its last sentence. It is chilling, but ultimately fulfills the enlightening effort of the whole book. Obviously, it forces us to confront the "Rashomon" aspect of experience—that

things look different to different observers, and that one's very perceptions are shaped by the social and cultural context out of which one
operates.   (3)

That about sums up the mission of *Things Fall Apart,* if a novel could be
said to have a mission.

TEACHING THE AUTHOR

Chinua Achebe and the Signs of the Times
Simon Gikandi

Because I often teach *Things Fall Apart* in a genre course that seeks to elaborate, question, and revise several key assumptions about the contemporary novel, especially the relation between language and ideology, my critical and pedagogical approach emphasizes the complex relations among authors, texts, and what V. Y. Mudimbe calls "epistemological contexts" (*Invention* ix). As a teacher of fiction, I recognize the dangers of interpretations anchored in an author's life, times, and thought. Students who see too close a parallel between a novelist's ideology and his or her thematic concerns tend to read the text solely from an authorial perspective. Indeed, every teacher of *Things Fall Apart* eventually confronts two important questions: Must students be familiar with Achebe's experiences and clearly articulated views of African history and culture to understand the novel's linguistic and narrative structures? When do such extratextual elements impede the student's ability to read the text in its own terms?

Clearly, the overwhelming weight of history and biography and the multiple cultural formations at work in *Things Fall Apart* make denying the truth-value of Achebe's novel a futile exercise. However, any unquestioned assumption that the text empirically reflects the author's experiences seduces students into reproducing their worst reading habits. My methodology is hence compelled by two factors: first, the need to stress the author's central position in contextualizing a work of fiction and providing a vital link between the sociological and aesthetic dimensions of the literary text; second, the need to wean my students from the persistent habit of allowing an author to limit the way they read texts, which often leads to paraphrasing rather than critical interpretation. In teaching Achebe's novel I encourage my students to go beyond the traditional view that novels naturally represent an author's life and times and to use Achebe's views and experiences as a point of entry into the deep structure of *Things Fall Apart*.

But readers face a still greater challenge in negotiating this relation between authors and texts—the need to deconstruct the dominant view of the African novel as a source of ethnographic data. Achebe presents particular problems in this regard because many of his pronouncements on African fiction seem to foster an anthropological approach that, in my view, forestalls a more complex reading of his works. It is difficult to discourage students from such a perspective when they have already heard Achebe claim, in an interview with Kalu Ogbaa, that he does not object if readers use his novels as sources of cultural information. According to Achebe, "[I]f someone is in search of information, or knowledge, or enlightenment about the total life of these people—the Igbo people—I think my novels would be a good source" (1). Although I do not oppose any sensible use of Achebe's fiction for its supply of cultural data, I caution my students that novels, like all sources of knowledge, proffer incomplete and often contradictory perspectives.

My major task in introducing students to *Things Fall Apart* is to provide a theoretical foundation for relating Achebe to his times without discussing his novel simply as an empirical record of Igbo culture or the African experience before and during the period of colonization. My goal is not to deny the validity of Achebe's claims about the sources of his novel but to complicate his pronouncements on culture and representation. For example, Achebe reports that he wrote *Things Fall Apart* from information garnered in his childhood, when he was able "to catch glimpses of what the complete traditional society must have looked like"; but he adds that he "supplemented these impressions with accounts, stories told by old people—like my father" (Duerden 9). The word *experience* has particular resonance in Achebe's reflections; I argue that it is a loaded term, referring not only to the author's conception of his culture but also to his indebtedness to stories told by other observers of Igbo culture.

Indeed, Achebe states, "[E]xperience is not simply what happened. . . . Experience is what we are able and prepared to do with what happens to us" (*Morning* xiii). While this assertion may not tell us much about Achebe's understanding of representation in fiction, it allows me to introduce my theoretical proposition, borrowed from Edward W. Said's *Orientalism*, that what is circulated and exchanged within a culture is not truth but representations. I carefully restate Said's claim that "in any instance of at least written language, there is no such thing as a delivered presence, but a *re-presence*, or a representation" (21). After I explain to students the difference between a delivered presence (which assumes that the experience in the text is original) and a representation (which posits experience as an effect of language, ideology, and narrative strategies), we discuss, and also modify, terms such as *self*, *language*, and *authorship*, which are central to understanding the novel as a genre.

Because our class is a genre course, I encourage students to read *Things Fall Apart* as a particular kind of contemporary novel—one written under the influence of high modernism but still relying on traditional nineteenth-century conventions of narration. To underscore the distinction between modern and traditional novels, I return to questions of authorship, this time from the perspective of critical theorists who define the contemporary novel as a work whose interpretation does not depend on the privileged position of its author. I quote Roland Barthes's notorious claim that "writing is the destruction of every voice, of every point of origin. Writing is that neutral, composite, oblique space where our subject slips away, the negative where all identity is lost, starting with the very identity of the body writing" (142). Since I have already stressed the extent to which Achebe values questions of voice and identity—indeed I argue that these are primary ideological concerns in the novel—my ostensibly approving citation of Barthes often confuses students.

I reassure the class that I really don't share Barthes's conviction that the death of the author is a precondition for modern writing; nevertheless, Barthes does provide a good case against modes of reading that are "tyrannically centred on the author" (143). As we begin our study of Achebe's text I pose two questions for my students to keep in mind: Does the presence of the author and our knowledge of his life, times, and ideas nourish our reading of his book? Or is Barthes right in his claim that "to give a text an Author is to impose a limit on that text, to furnish it with a final signified, to close the writing" (147)? I usually solicit student responses to these two questions before I introduce the concept of intertextuality as described by Barthes and Michel Foucault and relate it to the function of the author in the text. At this juncture I approvingly quote Barthes's claim that a text is not

> a line of words releasing a single "theological" meaning (the "message" of the Author-God) but a multi-dimensional space in which a variety of writings, none of them original, blend and clash. The text is a tissue of quotations drawn from the innumerable centres of culture.　(146)

However, to counter Barthes's statement I suggest that the author still dominates this space, in the words of Foucault, "as a historical figure at the crossroads of a certain number of events"; this figure "provides the basis for explaining not only the presence of certain events in a work, but also their transformations, distortions, and diverse modifications" (151).

These quotations naturally lead us to the crossroads metaphor in Achebe's aesthetic and autobiographical writings. I emphasize his assertions that his family "lived at the crossroads of cultures" and that "the crossroads does have a certain dangerous potency" (*Morning* 67). We then discuss Achebe's awareness of his position as a member of two cultures and the potential benefits and perils of that position; I stress the extent to which the crossroads represents what Jacques Derrida calls "a play of differences" (11). Such differences and tensions exist outside the text in Achebe's names (he had been christened Albert), his dual experiences as the son of a Christian and the grandson of an important man in Igbo traditional culture, and the contrast between colonial education and the oral traditions of the Igbo people. The text also manifests these tensions in the authorial ideologies that determine the way Achebe represents Igbo culture and in Okonkwo's tenuous position in what Achebe calls the Fanonist zone of "occult instability" (*Morning* 90).

When Achebe began writing his novel in the early 1950s, he was gripped by certain ideological and cultural anxieties about his relation to the decaying colonial culture and the emerging nationalist tradition. Achebe was privileged in the colonial order of things: his family was part of a new Christian elite that looked down on the traditionalists as the "people of nothing," he acquired literacy in the colonial language at an early age, and he went to Government College, Umuahia, one of the most selective institutions in the country. But, as I also tell my students, Achebe came of age at a time when African nationalists were challenging the dominance of the old colonial order; as colonial blessings began to appear mixed, members of the African elite were forced to reconsider their positions in relation to both colonialism and the traditional culture. Admitted as one of the first students at University College, Ibadan (Nigeria's first university, founded in 1948), Achebe abandoned his plans to study medicine, preferring instead to read English; he wanted to become a writer who could represent his people in other ways than they had been represented in colonial texts.

While I rarely attach much significance to such straightforward biographical facts, they help me make the point that *Things Fall Apart* is informed by Achebe's doubts about his status as a colonial subject and by what I call his nationalist desire—the need to defend an African culture and to will a Nigerian national consciousness into being. Discussing the writer's role in a new nation, for example, Achebe informs us that he began to write because he wanted to validate African culture in the face of colonial historiography. He wanted to show that "African people did not hear of culture for the first time from Europeans; that their societies were not mindless but frequently had a philosophy of great depth and value and beauty, that they had poetry and, above all, they had dignity" (Killam, *African Writers* 8). Consequently, in his quest for a new African narrative, Achebe believes that "the worst thing that can happen to any people is the loss of their dignity and self-respect"; the writer's duty "is to help them regain it by showing them in human terms what happened to them, what they lost" (8).

The text, of course, offers us many examples of the beauty, philosophy, and poetry of Igbo culture: the drama of the wrestling match that opens the novel, the signs that accompany greetings, and the rituals of harvest, marriage, and death. But Achebe is also concerned with the contradictions that inform Umuofian culture and the limitations of its ethos. He emphasizes the strains and distortions within this culture and, more important, its transformations under colonial occupation; he wants to represent the dualities of the Igbo value system that make culture possible. In this respect, the ambiguous position of Okonkwo as a cultural hero warrants some discussion. I usually point out that we can define Achebe's subject as tragic precisely because Okonkwo is exiled and because he eventually kills himself in defense of Umuofia's "masculine" values. Why, I often ask my students, does a novel that opens with the celebration of a cultural hero end with such an unprecedented act of transgression?

In a further lecture on the origins of *Things Fall Apart*, I describe the novel's awareness of the colonial narratives that precede it, narratives that it seeks to revise or negate. Once again, we examine Achebe's views on the influence these narratives have had on his work. I refer my students to several essays in which Achebe specifically discusses the ideologies and discursive strategies embedded in some influential colonial texts—namely Joyce Cary's *Mister Johnson* and Joseph Conrad's *Heart of Darkness*—that he encountered as a student at Ibadan. Achebe's literary education, I remind my students, was dominated by traditional Western literary texts and nonfictional European writings on Africa, what he once called "the sedate prose of the district-officer-government anthropologist of sixty or seventy years ago" (*Morning* 5); to produce a narrative that would subvert this discourse, he first had to read the European texts differently. I support this contention with a quote from a recent interview with Bill Moyers in which Achebe describes how his previous reading of colonial texts—and his identification with "the good white man" against "African savages"—was transformed:

> In the university I suddenly saw that these books had to be read in a different light. Reading *Heart of Darkness* . . . I realized that I was one of those savages jumping up and down on the beach. Once that kind of enlightenment comes to you, you realize that someone has to write a different story. And since I was in any case inclined that way, why not me? (343)

In what ways, I ask, does Achebe's novel constitute a different story—a counternarrative to the European texts? If students are familiar with Conrad's novel, we discuss the different ways in which Achebe and Conrad represent African cultures and the African landscape. If students are not familiar with Conrad, I quickly summarize *Heart of Darkness* and then provide detailed textual examples of *Things Fall Apart* as a response to the colonial text; I spend considerable time showing the narrative techniques Achebe adopts to contest the silent shadows and forms of colonialist discourse. In the opening paragraph of the novel, for example, Achebe seems to eschew exaggeration in his descriptions of Umuofia, representing the drama of the wrestling match in simple and ordinary prose. The narrator chooses a restrained mode of narration to counter the exotic descriptions we find in both Conrad and Cary.

Furthermore, in his representation of Umuofia, the narrator deliberately seeks to restore to the African character three elements that are missing in colonial narratives, namely subjectivity, history, and voice. The novel opens by evoking a unique subject (Okonkwo), who exists in a functioning cultural and temporal context (Umuofia). While most colonial narratives seem to cut off the African character from representation—especially from concrete historical and social circumstances—Achebe's text is dominated by a sense of things happening according to the movement of time. *Things Fall Apart* is the narrative of a community where "everyone speaks from a somewhere which always indicates a historicity, a becoming, and their questions" (Mudimbe, "Real Thing" 316). Time, I tell my students, is an important constitutive principle of the novel as a genre; it often triggers a multiplicity of oppositions between character and society, nature and culture, movement and stasis. I provide examples of such oppositions in the novel.

By this time, of course, I find myself discussing Achebe and the narrator as if they were interchangeable. My final lecture on the novel seeks to complicate the relation between author and narrator before I raise the issues of voice and representation, which are crucial to understanding the novel. Here, a useful strategy is to summarize several of the debates about narrative voice in Achebe's novel. While some readers assume that Achebe is the speaker in the novel, I remind my students that he may not be and that no critical consensus exists on the issue: one critic identifies the speaker as "a wise and sympathetic elder of the tribe" (Carroll 37), while another declares that the narrator re-creates a voice similar to that of "the epic poet whose society is as yet unproblematic" (Innes and Lindfors 112).

I allow students to discuss the merits of such claims before I suggest, using numerous textual examples, that the narrator's position, identity, and perspective change often in the novel. *Things Fall Apart* represents Igbo culture through different voices and perspectives, but what is important about such voices is not whether they are right or wrong but that they are generated from within the culture itself. Although a European mode of representation (writing) triumphs at the end of the novel, Achebe gives voice to his culture; thus his novel functions as "an act of atonement with [his] past, the ritual return and homage of a prodigal son" (*Morning* 70).

Following the Author in *Things Fall Apart*

Emmanuel Obiechina

My advice to the teacher of *Things Fall Apart* is simple, just three words: follow the author. Because the novel takes place in the past and in an African community, students may find aspects of its world and its cultural values unfamiliar. Teachers may also be handicapped by unfamiliarity; indeed, many critical works about the novel address this need by providing background information. But even without such studies, notes, and commentaries, or in spite of them, perceptive teachers who follow the verbal signposts established by the author within the narrative should find the novel accessible. Unlike many other novels, *Things Fall Apart* provides its own notes and commentaries and does not even seem to need its glossary.

In this novel, Chinua Achebe is quintessentially a teacher. George Eliot sees the novelist as a "teacher or influencer of the public mind" (Allott 94), but Achebe's role as teacher goes beyond influencing the public mind—or the public's moral taste or the action of the intelligence. For Achebe, literature is a form of communication requiring the transference of experience from the author to the reader. In *Things Fall Apart*, Achebe is preoccupied not only with the experience itself but also with the best manner of conveying it. He anticipates likely difficulties for the reader and attempts to resolve them by using well-chosen strategies of technique and language. Teachers who follow the author's lead can navigate the world and experience contained in the novel without too much strain.

Achebe is, of course, aware that he uses his works to educate the reader. In an essay titled "The Novelist as Teacher," he defines his role graphically:

> Here then is an adequate revolution for me to espouse—to help my society regain belief in itself and put away the complexes of the years of denigration and self-abasement. And it is essentially a question of education, in the best sense of that word. . . . I would be quite satisfied if my novels (especially the ones I set in the past) did no more than teach my readers that their past—with all its imperfections—was not one long night of savagery from which the first Europeans acting on God's behalf delivered them. (*Morning* 44–45)

Teachers of *Things Fall Apart* should know this essay because it throws light on Achebe's intentions in the novel. He sets out to remove misunderstandings and to restore the truth of a way of life that has been misrepresented over the centuries. Achebe scrupulously pursues the truth of the characters' humanity, and he is wholly sensitive to the historical, cultural, and psychological impulses operating on the characters and their society. The fundamental role he has set for himself as an African novelist readily explains his choice of title, themes, and creative stances.

As explainer and teacher, Achebe positions himself strategically, at a vantage point from which he sees everything, in order to explain everything. He is the controlling consciousness of the narrative, "the Watcher," as Henry James would describe him (Allott 131–32). His guiding hand directs the action, deploys emphases, defines relevances, and assesses the ethical qualities of individual and group conduct throughout the novel. He also corrects misrepresentations and distorted views of the characters and their society.

So important is the task of education to the author that he presses one of his characters, Obierika, into service as a secondary center of consciousness. Obierika, the friend of Okonkwo, is close to the center of the action. Yet he differs so much from the hero that he almost serves as a foil. As a philosophical, moral man whose views and comments always deserve respect, he provides the voice of reason and sobriety. Deeply exposed to the traditional life of Umuofia, Obierika understands it in great detail, in its triumphant and tragic aspects, in its strengths and weaknesses. Apart from the author, Obierika is the most reliable guide in *Things Fall Apart*, a role Achebe deliberately assigns him. Teachers should recognize and exploit the novel's two sources of authoritative guidance, and both teacher and students should test their interpretations of the novel against the insights provided by these sources.

First and foremost, the teacher of *Things Fall Apart* should determine through close textual study the verbal signposts the author uses to convey his insights. The most important signposts are the key statements that develop a large part of the novel's action and character exploration. Often the author edges in such statements as if they were not important, when instead they constitute the pivots on which much else depends. Readers unattentive to Achebe's organizational strategies may overlook these signposts because they are intrusive rather than obtrusive. For example, in the book's first paragraph, which describes the famous wrestling match between young Okonkwo and Amalinze the Cat, Achebe comments that Okonkwo's "fame rested on solid personal achievements" (3). This sentence could easily be lost as the novel moves on to describe the life of Okonkwo's father, and yet the statement is central to unraveling the hero's character. The author includes several similar statements: "And he did pounce on people quite often," "[h]e had no patience with unsuccessful men," "[h]e had had no patience with his father," "his whole life was dominated by fear, the fear of failure and of weakness" (3, 9). These kernels around which the author builds the hero's character represent what I call the intrusive mode of Achebe's verbal signposts. Achebe subsequently fleshes out and dramatizes these keynote statements in different contexts. Indeed, like the controlling tones in a musical symphony, these statements are played and replayed in a variety of pitches, harmonies, melodies, and rhythms because of their strategic importance in the total scheme of character and social explorations.

Thus, Achebe elaborates the statement that Okonkwo's fame is based on solid personal achievements in a number of contexts on subsequent pages. So firmly established is this aspect of the hero's identity that when another character, displeased with Okonkwo's lack of humility, suggests that his success is a matter of luck, the author intervenes to correct the misrepresentation: "If ever a man deserved his success, that man was Okonkwo" (19), asserts the authorial voice, and it proceeds to enumerate his accomplishments. Okonkwo is a flawed hero, but Achebe does not want him blamed for the wrong reasons.

The statement that Okonkwo "did pounce on people quite often" provides another example of Achebe's technique (3). Several incidents bear out this comment: Okonkwo breaks the sacred Week of Peace by beating his youngest wife (21), he beats and takes a shot at his second wife (27–28), he cuts down Ikemefuna in the fatal bush (43), he murderously beats his son Nwoye for going to Christian services (107), and he impulsively beheads the court messenger before hanging himself (144). Impulsive violence is an aspect of his character. If we add to this trait the fact that anger is the only emotion the hero is capable of experiencing, we have the picture of an impetuous and violent man doomed to fall, in spite of his great personal achievements.

The author establishes his signposts so clearly that he leaves no ambiguities or ethical fluidities in matters requiring definite and precise judgment. In Ikemefuna's death, for example, several ethical conditions are at issue. Ikemefuna's life at Umuofia is full of pathos, but the author makes it clear that readers need to separate the pity they feel for a young child caught in the complexities of adult politics from their evaluation of that politics. Another consideration is the morality of Okonkwo's participation in the murder of a child who regards him as a father.

References to Ikemefuna occur many times in connection with the hero's personal achievements:

> As the elders said, if a child washed his hands he could eat with kings. Okonkwo had clearly washed his hands and so he ate with kings and elders. And that was how he came to look after the doomed lad who was sacrificed to the village of Umuofia by their neighbours to avoid war and bloodshed. The ill-fated lad was called Ikemefuna.   (6)

Elsewhere, we learn that the war threatening the peaceful relations between Mbaino and Umuofia is a just war, ratified by the communal assembly and sanctioned by the oracle. Okonkwo is the emissary who carries the ultimatum to the enemy:

> And so when Okonkwo of Umuofia arrived at Mbaino as the proud and imperious emissary of war, he was treated with great honour and

respect, and two days later he returned home with a lad of fifteen and a young virgin. The lad's name was Ikemefuna, whose sad story is still told in Umuofia unto this day.   (9)

Ikemefuna is also linked to Okonkwo's standing in the community:

At the most one could say that [Okonkwo's] *chi* or personal god was good. But the Ibo people have a proverb that when a man says yes his *chi* says yes also. Okonkwo said yes very strongly; so his *chi* agreed. And not only his *chi* but his clan too, because it judged a man by the work of his hands. That was why Okonkwo had been chosen by the nine villages to carry a message of war to their enemies unless they agreed to give up a young man and a virgin to atone for the murder of Udo's wife. And such was the deep fear that their enemies had for Umuofia that they treated Okonkwo like a king and brought him a virgin who was given to Udo as wife, and the lad Ikemefuna.
                                                                        (19–20)

Even though these passages appear repetitious, they are not. Each differs contextually and has additional layers of information that clarify one aspect or another of the narrative. The first quotation broadly states Ikemefuna's status. The boy is not a war hostage but a sacrificial victim given by his people to atone for his father's murder of the Umuofia woman. The author's choice of words provides the insight. Achebe refers to Ikemefuna as "the doomed lad who was sacrificed to the village of Umuofia by their neighbours to avoid war and bloodshed" and as "the ill-fated lad." In the third passage the phrase "to atone for the murder of Udo's wife" underlines Ikemefuna's judicial-sacrificial destiny. This idea is so important that Achebe repeats it in the context of Okonkwo's report to the elders:

The elders, or *ndichie*, met to hear a report of Okonkwo's mission. At the end they decided, as everybody knew they would, that the girl should go to Ogbuefi Udo to replace his murdered wife. As for the boy, he belonged to the clan as a whole, and there was no hurry to decide his fate. Okonkwo was, therefore, asked on behalf of the clan to look after him in the interim. And so for three years Ikemefuna lived in Okonkwo's household.   (9)

The author devotes ample attention to the issue of war and peace. Laws and conventions exist for regulating conflicts among peoples. In Umuofia, determining whether a war is just has such significance that it is vested in the Oracle of the Hills and the Caves who, when necessary, forbids the people from going into "*a fight of blame*" (9). If the war is to be just, people must follow the proper conventions and first attempt to settle the issue amicably, such as by exacting a reparation. If peaceful methods fail, the society makes a formal declaration of war. In the quotation, the intruded clause "as everybody knew they would" underscores the existence of the law of war between neighbors. Again, the fact that "there was no hurry to decide his fate" shows that the matter does not involve personal feeling. Chapter 7 begins:

> For three years Ikemefuna lived in Okonkwo's household and the elders of Umuofia seemed to have forgotten about him.   (37)

No one seems eager to terminate Ikemefuna's young life. But if the elders have forgotten about him, the ever-vigilant oracle has not, and so, at the appropriate time, it moves against him.

But while the author justifies the clan's action as following tradition, he condemns Okonkwo's participation in Ikemefuna's murder. The text provides abundant evidence of Achebe's position, emphasizing Ikemefuna's integration into Okonkwo's household and the warm relationship between the boy and Okonkwo that makes Okonkwo's action unnatural. Even though Okonkwo treats him "with a heavy hand," as he treats everyone else, the author informs us that

> there was no doubt that he liked the boy. Sometimes when he went to big village meetings or communal ancestral feasts he allowed Ikemefuna to accompany him, like a son, carrying his stool and his goatskin bag. And, indeed, Ikemefuna called him father.   (20)

This bond is not lost on the thoughtful elders. When the time comes for Ikemefuna to be killed, the oldest man in Okonkwo's village visits Okonkwo to warn him against being involved: "That boy calls you father. Do not bear a hand in his death" (40). Okonkwo ignores the warning and actually cuts the boy down when he runs to him for protection in the fatal bush, crying, "My father, they have killed me!" (43).

Obierika condemns Okonkwo's action:

> If I were you I would have stayed at home. What you have done will not please the Earth. It is the kind of action for which the goddess wipes out whole families.   (46)

Okonkwo's excuse—that he only carried out the earth-mother goddess's command—is not convincing. Obierika offers the more convincing and morally sound view that, should the oracle demand the death of his son, Obierika would neither dispute the oracle's wish nor be the one to carry it out.

Obierika provides significant insights in the later part of the novel, particularly after Okonkwo goes into exile for unintentionally killing Ezeudu's son. Obierika sees the punishment as far too heavy for the offense, but as a good traditionalist he tries to accommodate it. It is easy to see why the author, who reports Obierika's perception with approval, uses him as a center of consciousness:

> Obierika was a man who thought about things. When the will of the goddess had been done, he sat down in his *obi* and mourned his friend's calamity. Why should a man suffer so grievously for an offence he had committed inadvertently? But although he thought for a long time he found no answer. He was merely led into greater complexities. He remembered his wife's twin children, whom he had thrown away. What crime had they committed? The Earth had decreed that they were an offence on the land and must be destroyed. And if the clan did not exact punishment for an offence against the great goddess, her wrath was loosed on all the land and not just on the offender. As the elders said, if one finger brought oil it soiled the others.   (87)

When Okonkwo returns to Umuofia after his years of exile, so much has changed that the old society is hardly recognizable. Obierika offers an invaluable and completely reliable picture of the collapse of tradition in an effort to help Okonkwo see the futility of armed resistance to the new forces:

> It is already too late. . . . Our own men and our sons have joined the ranks of the stranger. . . . How do you think we can fight when our own brothers have turned against us? The white man is very clever. He came quietly and peaceably with his religion. We were amused at his foolishness and allowed him to stay. Now he has won our brothers, and our clan can no longer act like one. He has put a knife on the things that held us together and we have fallen apart.   (124–25)

But Okonkwo's inner weaknesses and some external factors combine to neutralize the effect of such a sensible appeal, and the hero plunges deep into his disaster. Finally, Obierika provides the hero's epitaph:

> That man was one of the greatest men in Umuofia. You drove him to kill himself; and now he will be buried like a dog.   (147)

Things Fall Apart reveals Achebe's integrity, knowledge, and historical and cultural visions, particularly in its handling of the central themes of cultural conflict and change. His understanding of the traditional agrarian culture works to build an impressive picture of its social, political, economic, and religious institutions and values; its arts and crafts; and its modes of perceiving reality. Achebe's representation of that society is so clearly and comprehensively drawn that, when the new forces begin to impinge on it and to undermine its stability, the reader can easily follow the drama.

In painting this picture of the traditional way of life, Achebe justly describes not only the positive aspects but also the negative ones. He sidesteps the temptation to idealize or romanticize that way of life. Teachers and students of *Things Fall Apart* should trust Achebe's perspective and adopt a close reading of his novel, paying particular attention to the verbal signposts through which the author clarifies his themes. Readers should also note Obierika's views and observations with care, because the author uses Obierika to convey some of the novel's finest insights. By testing their views and interpretations against those of the author and of Obierika, teachers and students enjoy the benefit of the author's excellent pedagogical design.

TEACHING CONTEXT

Things Fall Apart in Its Time and Place

Robert M. Wren

Students may have difficulty approaching *Things Fall Apart* because they know little about African history and nothing at all about the history of southeastern Nigeria, the locale of the novel. The novel seems abstracted in time and place, a mythic Africa, even though Achebe roots the characters and action in a realistic, if fictional, world. Achebe's world is not mythic and should not be seen as such. Viewing Okonkwo's predicament as part of an ongoing historical process is important to the author's intention: Achebe wants to demonstrate that Europe did not bring "civilization" to "savages" (unless one accepts the older European senses of both words); he wants to show that civil order existed in a framework of tradition, political understanding, and faith. That framework falls apart under the rule of European strangers. A closely integrated society with a common will—a community in the truest, richest sense of that word—loses its integrity when the Europeans take over. The invaders cannot appreciate the society they have "infected with individualism."

The novel takes place at the beginning of the twentieth century, when British authorities, missions, and trade penetrated the Igbo hinterland east of the Niger River. The society described in part 1 is civil and ordered. To this society, in part 2, come the colonial officer and the missionary, invaders as incomprehensible as they are uncomprehending. With them come still other strangers, Africans from far and near, who do the colonial bidding as soldiers, messengers, agents, and teachers. These invaders render the traditional mechanisms of order ineffective, and, as a result, the novel's community, Umuofia, becomes confused and divided. Okonkwo, the central character, falls victim to the confusion and hangs himself, an abomination. The District Commissioner, after but a moment's thought, resolves to note the event in the book he is writing, *The Pacification of the Primitive Tribes of the Lower Niger.*

The words *pacification* and *primitive* are used with great irony at the end of the novel. My approach to *Things Fall Apart* uses these two concepts as keys to understanding both the novel and the culture that Achebe invites his readers to share.

Students and teachers need to look at two larger histories. One is the unfamiliar and unexpected reality of centuries of life and action among the people of the lands portrayed in the novel. This history needs less explication because the novel itself is its testimonial. The other history—more familiar, perhaps, yet little known—is the European "scramble for Africa" that took place in the nineteenth century. One of the many results of this movement was that Britain secured control of the great, populous, and varied territory that now constitutes the nation called Nigeria.

That territory has never had any integrity save one imposed by the colonial powers. Hundreds of different ethnic and linguistic communities are crushed into one "nation." The largest of these communities are those of the Hausa-speaking peoples (among whom are other, bilingual peoples) of the northern regions of Nigeria. The Yoruba of the southwest make up the second largest group, and third in numbers are the Igbo of the southeast. The Igbo are, collectively, Achebe's own people, but they are not homogeneous. "Igbo" villages only a few miles apart once spoke languages—all called "Igbo"— that were as different as German and Dutch are in northern Europe. (Education and other forces are blending out the differences, leading to what may in time become a unified Igbo language.) The dialects, cultures, and political systems of Igbo east of the great Niger River are unlike those of the Igbo on the western side. And, if we may leap over several other, smaller ethnicities, Igbo language and culture radically depart from those of the Yoruba in the southwest—as much as, say, German does from Italian. At the same time, Yoruba and Igbo cultures differ from northern Nigerian Hausa cultures even more greatly—as much, perhaps, as British culture differs from Russian. The conquerors crushed all this diversity into a single nation.

The "pacification," as it is ironically identified at the end of the novel, occurred between 1900 and 1920, a time span that roughly indicates the period from the start of the action of *Things Fall Apart* to the beginning of Achebe's third novel, *Arrow of God.* The first movement of conquest, a campaign against an Igbo people called the Aro in the far southeast of Igboland, began early in December 1901 and continued into January 1902. According to J. C. Anene, the British believed that the destruction of the Aro's great oracle would break a perceived Aro political hegemony and open all the hinterland to colonization. Anene shows that the British were wrong. True, many villages did accept the newcomers, but they were not villages ruled by the Aro. Many others did not know or did not care about British power or were unfriendly or were uncomprehending (231–37). The fictional Abame, site of a massacre reported early in part 2 of *Things Fall Apart*, provides an example of a village that did not understand British power. The Abame slaughter paved the way for a more peaceful invasion of Umuofia and neighboring villages by colonial officers and missionaries. The same process occurred at and around an actual town, Ahiara. Ahiara was one of many Igbo towns "punished" (in the colonial term) for resistance after the supposed success of the Aro expedition. (The last "collective punishment" took place long after Ahiara, in 1920.)

The facts of the Ahiara massacre closely conform to Obierika's account of the Abame incident. On 16 November 1905, J. F. Stewart, traveling by bicycle from Owerri, missed his way, fell into unfriendly hands, and was killed. A. E. Afigbo found that the Ahiara people "took him to their neighbours . . . to show *what* they had caught," because "they did not know he was a human being" (*Warrant Chiefs* 67). Nearly a month later, according to Colonial Office records, a Captain Fox leading two groups of black soldiers (each probably with a white officer) visited Ahiara briefly but found few people. Some days later, returning troops slaughtered many people in villages where Stewart was thought to have been held. Four hundred seventy-one locally made guns (like Okonkwo's inaccurate piece in the novel) were confiscated, and, probably, the towns themselves were burned ("Southern Nigeria"; "Southern Nigeria Dispatches"). The novel and history meet.

Achebe knew the story of Ahiara; it was famous because Stewart's death was the pretext for the Bende-Onitsha hinterland expedition, which destroyed an oracle at Awka, subdued the Ahiaras and other resistant groups, and opened the way for motor-road construction. This second British campaign, much more than the Aro expedition, made the land accessible to British government officials and missionaries. Abame symbolizes this conquest, and the true story, like Achebe's fiction, explains why relatively few towns risked government wrath. Surprisingly, a few towns and a few men did resist, defying the power of the British authorities to the end.

Subjection by indiscriminate slaughter and terror, with indifference to individual guilt or local law, was illegal and a contradiction of traditional British justice. However, no one knew how else to subdue these Igbo towns. Each was independent of every other town, and each was ruled by a consensus of leading citizens—as in Umuofia—and not by an autocratic chief. The long-term effect of rule by terror was to make the British settlers sacred (or at least sacrosanct); in *No Longer at Ease* Achebe comments, of a later period, "To throw a white man was like unmasking an ancestral spirit" (65). It was not only not done, it was not thought of.

African agents of the British were protected similarly, whether they were Igbo from distant places or local Christian converts, like the hothead Enoch in the novel. Of the colonial agents the worst were the court messengers, or *kotma*, true individualists without loyalty to any person or principle save self-interest—the perfect opposite of Igbo collective mores. Many of these *kotma*, Achebe says, were from Umuru, the name the novel gives to Onitsha, the great trading center on the high east bank of the Niger. The Church Missionary Society (Anglican) and the Holy Ghost Fathers (Roman Catholic) set up the first hinterland Igbo mission stations and schools there. The missionaries attracted Onitsha's alien commercial community: migrants lured by money, they became traders who adapted to the changes and created what would in time become the greatest market in western Africa. The more devout students of the missionaries became mission agents; many others became clerks to civil government or to European authorities; the less successful students (or the less scrupulous) might become court messengers, responsible for carrying messages from district officers to the local chiefs. They could not function as mere messengers, however, because the democratic Igbo villages did not recognize chiefs. As a result, *kotma* became colonial police to the disorderly democracies, those same democracies that had policed themselves successfully for as long as memory could reach. In the novel, *kotma* bring men for trial, guard the prison, beat the prisoners, demand bribes of them, and force men of honor to do degrading work. Although hated, they nevertheless share the almost sacred protection given the British, which is why the townspeople are astonished that Okonkwo would, at a critical moment, kill one.

The British understood obedience to orders; the Igbo people did not. The Igbo understood open discussion and collective rule; the British did not. The colonial officers did not know Igbo, and the elders of the towns did not know English. Both sides were forced to work through interpreters who— to make bad matters worse—were *kotma* or of the same individualistic kind as *kotma* and were prone to bribery, as Achebe says in chapter 20. (In Achebe's *Man of the People*, a former interpreter, Odili's father, is hated but rich by local standards.) The district commissioner in *Things Fall Apart* supports the ruthlessness of the *kotma*. Treacherously, the Commissioner invites the leading men of Umuofia to a "palaver." When they are unarmed and seated, the *kotma* arrest them. Again Achebe is true to history. Such deception of honorable citizens was a common practice, though some British colonial officers protested against it as early as 1900 (Afigbo, *Warrant Chiefs* 69).

The British brought injustice. That, however, was not their only disruptive contribution. They also brought trade, a major element in the imagined process of "civilization" that the British believed they were giving to savages. In Umuofia, Achebe says in chapter 21, "palm-oil and kernel became things of great price" (126). The palm, the abundant source of this wealth, was virtually a gift from nature; the technology of extracting the oil was, along with cultivation of the yam, a prime basis for life in the tropical forest region, where yam and palm oil were the staples of all diets, soap was made from oil and ashes, and oil was burned in lamps and worn as a cosmetic and as a dressing for the hair. In England, the oil's major use was to lubricate the machines of industry (it was also an ingredient in domestic products, like soap). In Africa, the villagers spent their new wealth on imports from Europe—cotton cloth, tobacco, beads, gin, porcelain plates, and iron pots.

Trade, government, and religion were the colonial trinity, and the greatest of these was the dominant European religion, Christianity. In the novel, Christianity is still at its first stage, that of winning converts. Investigating Achebe's account of the conversions, Afigbo reports that it may "with appropriate caution, be treated as containing reliable historical information" (*Warrant Chiefs* 66). The new faith, Achebe and Afigbo agree, attracted the alienated members of the community, the misfits, and the outcasts. Only slowly did persons of dignity and respect adopt the new faith.

Like Nwoye in the novel, Achebe's father was a convert. In the essay "Named for Victoria, Queen of England," Achebe writes that his father, Isaiah Achebe, was an orphan raised by his maternal grandfather, Udo Osinyi. Unlike Nwoye, who argued with Okonkwo, Isaiah Achebe did not leave his grandfather because of a quarrel. Isaiah Achebe was a true convert. His teacher and mentor was a missionary named G. T. Basden, whom Achebe has immortalized as Mr. Brown in the novel. Basden, like Brown, was a patient man, ready to discuss theology with non-Christians; like Brown, Basden was presented with an elephant tusk in appreciation of a quarter century of service in the Onitsha-Ogidi-Awka area, which is Achebe's home ground. Basden reported his discoveries in two books, the richer of which is titled *Niger Ibos*. Not surprisingly, descriptions of ceremonies in *Things Fall Apart* are often close to Basden's: both writers learned the traditions of Achebe's home, Ogidi—Basden as sympathetic visitor, Achebe as indigene.

The religion of Umuofia was, to Basden, superstition—primitive but interesting, like the "bad bush" (Evil Forest in the novel) into which twins and other abominations (like Okonkwo's father) were put to die (Basden 58). When missionaries lived in the "bad bush" and survived, they seemed to prove the power of the new religion. To Achebe, of course, the old religion is more than interesting; the Oracle of the Hills and the Caves, for example, plays a vital role in the novel. Basden's discussion of oracles goes beyond anthropological commentary, condemning them as frauds, as priestly deceptions designed to bilk the credulous of wealth, freedom, and life. The oracle in Achebe's novel does not match Basden's characterization, but it surely is related to two that Achebe knew, one at the adjacent town of

Ogbunike and the other at his mother's home in Awka. K. Onwuka Dike follows Sidney R. Smith (a missionary who, with Basden, worked in the Ogidi area) in identifying Ogbunike not as a source of help, as in the novel, but merely as a source of slaves (40). Not long ago, while visiting the oracle Ogba, a cave in the Nkisi stream, I was told by a small boy how, in the old days, the guilty met two fates in the cave, one apparent, one real. The apparent fate was death, for blood would appear in the stream to deceive anxious waiting relatives. The blood, the boy told me, was chicken blood, for the priests did not kill their victims but instead took them captive and sold them to Aro traders. My guide scurried among labyrinthine entrances and exits to show how the priests might perplex supplicants before betraying them. This story matches the one Basden tells about the oracles. The only exception was the oracle he knew best, from long service in the Awka area. At Awka's oracle, he says, the guilty were in fact killed. Further, he says that the oracle was consulted for blessings and charms. The Awka oracle was called Agbala (82), the same name Achebe gives to the Oracle of the Hills and the Caves—Agbala, to whom people "came when misfortune dogged their steps . . . or to discover what the future held for them or to consult the spirits of their departed fathers" (12). Fiction is surely the better testimony.

Discussion of oracles opens the way to the other great history, that of the falsely labeled "primitive" world of the Igbo past, before the coming of the British. I briefly describe only two aspects of that history here: the system of titles that dominates masculine life in Umuofia and the dedication of people to gods, or *osu*.

The *ozo* titles are associated with an ancient society that was probably a thousand or more years old in 1900. In Umuofia, as in all the communities in a large region encompassing most of today's Anambra State, the *ozo* titles are held in the highest respect. Okonkwo grows up disgraced by his father, who never took a title and was therefore less than a man. Okonkwo's ambition is to take the highest titles in the land, and his failure to do so accounts in part for the anger that takes him to his death and shame. The origin of the *ozo* titles is lost in the past, available only by conjecture. The evidence hints that, long ago, the region was led by the king-priests of Nri, who were arbitrators of great disputes, loci of the highest priestly powers, and exclusive creators and owners of the *ozo* title. Whatever *ozo* titles a community might devise, the elementary ceremony by which a citizen became a full man could be sanctified only by the priests of Nri. The *ozo* title was no mere honor. It united a man with his ancestors; with an *ozo* title a man became immortal, a living god. He could achieve this position by accumulating wealth and honor (rarely, honor alone was enough, and sometimes wealth might do); the wealth was necessary because the initiate had to reward every person in the community who held the *ozo* title.

In the sacred city of Nri, which lies east of Achebe's home in Ogidi and south of Awka, certain treasures identified with Igbo-Ukwu have been excavated (Shaw, *Igbo-Ukwu* 268–70). Artifacts discovered there demonstrate the existence of a high culture and extensive trade, probably by the ninth century (Christian calendar) and extending for several hundred years. Conflict with the Aro may have brought the Nri hegemony to its end (Wren, *Achebe's World* 87–89). Nri provided the leadership that created the village societies of which Achebe writes. Their stability was ensured by Nri's spiritual (not military) enforcement of the rites of Ani, the earth goddess, and the granting of *ozo* titles. Each higher grade of *ozo* title required the distribution of greater wealth, so that no man became too rich or too powerful to control—no man could become a king, and every capable man with an *ozo* title was a god.

Against the high role of the *ozo* titles Achebe sets the painful reality of *osu*. Below both the free citizens and their slaves (the latter only alluded to in chapter 6) were the outcasts, the *osu*, people dedicated to a god as a kind of living sacrifice. From the moment of their sacrifice, the *osu* and their descendants became all but untouchable. The *osu* in the novel are among the first converts to the new church, a church that teaches the unity of all people and offers hope to victims of society's rigid forms. Like the antagonism that Okonkwo feels toward his father, and that Nwoye feels even more strongly toward Okonkwo, the *osu* represent a weakness, a subtle flaw in the structure of the Igbo world—a flaw that makes it possible for things to fall apart.

Understanding the historical context can help students see that the society of *Things Fall Apart*, which at first appears to be a seamless community that might have existed unchanged for an eternity, is something quite different. Its fragility, covertly shown in part 1, slowly becomes obvious when Umuofia is subjected to the rack of colonial injustice and when the traditional society's fragmented power is tested by the new religion that dares to live in the Evil Forest and survives. Behind the community and facing it is history. Achebe captures history in a few crucial years, the years that shaped the present most decisively for the people of southeastern Nigeria.

The Igbo as Exceptional Colonial Subjects: Fictionalizing an Abnormal Historical Situation

Dan Izevbaye

In *Things Fall Apart*, Achebe provides a cultural history designed to counter the myths and prejudices many readers have about Africans and the Igbo in particular. Achebe tackles the myth that colonialism merely disturbed secluded, provincial worlds by exposing them to the modern (that is, European) world with its advanced technology and complex institutions. He adopts the myth of Igbo isolation but rejects the idea that Igbo culture is necessarily primitive because of this isolation. While the novel is essentially an account of the Igbo past, it acts as a form of education through which the novelist as teacher might correct current misperceptions of African history and the contemporary status of African culture. This consciousness of the present serves as an important background for the novel. The colonial perception of Africans and their civilization, as reflected in European literature and ethnography, so affected the social and psychological state of Africans that Achebe must retell the story of the African past to educate Europeans and Africans alike. Thus, Achebe's novel is not meant to be autonomous, and the background is not simply the reality from which Achebe organized his text: the author elevates the background to a kind of subtext to which we relate the literary experience as we read. He injects just enough cultural information and explanation into the narrative to make the reader sense an underlying questioning of contemporary European views of Igbo history.

Although Achebe keeps the characters and the setting of the action fictional, he remains faithful to the historicity of the action itself. The novel thus preserves the essential features of Igbo history and, by extension, African history, at the point of contact with colonizing Europe. At the same time, the novel does not support the colonial misconception that all African cultures are alike. It serves primarily as a story of Igbo experience rather than as a typical account of African culture. While the story may fit the general pattern of cultural change in Africa, its details suggest that the Igbo were different—and knew they were different—from many of their neighbors. Okonkwo even speaks of a strange kinship and inheritance custom among a distant people (presumably the Akan people, who lived a thousand kilometers to the west, in what was soon to become the British Gold Coast): " 'The world is large,' said Okonkwo. 'I have even heard that in some tribes a man's children belong to his wife and her family' " (51). Readers should note that *Things Fall Apart* is not just a story of cultural contact; indeed, the District Commissioner does not appear till late in the story, after the rise and the beginning of the decline of Okonkwo. Although the story shows how the religious and economic activities of the Europeans change the culture of Umuofia, the narrative concludes with a comment—the District Commissioner's book title—directed not at the Europeans' culture but at their limited understanding of those they describe as the primitive tribes of the lower Niger.

Achebe adapted the tentative title of the District Commissioner's book from the titles of books by A. G. Leonard (1906) and G. T. Basden (1938). The title, *The Pacification of the Primitive Tribes of the Lower Niger*, is Achebe's critical allusion to the policy and practice of the British colonial government that ruled the Northern and Southern Protectorates of Nigeria (as they were then called) before they were amalgamated. British colonies in Africa were administered by indirect rule, a policy that required a study of the social organization and the political institutions of the people to be governed. The colonial administrations accumulated such a mass of information in their intelligence reports and other field studies of the different ethnic groups that many of these documents continue to serve scholars as important historical sources. But while these sources seemed adequate to the British administration, they did not appear to have helped the colonial administrators to a sympathetic understanding of certain "native institutions." What the reports revealed about the "Niger Ibos," for example, did not conform to British ideas of government and civil order. Civilization, for the British, meant a hierarchy of authority, a centralized system of rule, and, better still, a cultural link with a northerly, non-African people. Nowhere does this prejudice show more clearly than in Frederick Lugard's *Report on the Amalgamation of Northern and Southern Nigeria, 1912–1919*:

> The Southern Provinces were [mostly] populated by tribes in the lowest stage of primitive savagery, without any central organisation. . . . A great part of the North, on the other hand, had come under the influence of Islam, and . . . had an elaborate administrative machinery.
> (Qtd. in Kirk-Greene 67)

This "primitive savagery" of the peoples of the Southern Protectorate was thought to arise from their isolation since, according to European theory at the time, intercultural contact and dispersal were among the sources of civilization.

The intelligence reports by British administrators brought out the broad differences in the histories and social institutions of the ethnic communities occupying the territories both to the far north of the Niger and Benue rivers and below the confluence. The British colonizers found it more convenient, however, to govern the whole area as a single administrative unit treated as a cultural entity. The policy of indirect rule was based largely on the character of the Northern Protectorate, but it was determined by a British conception of civilization. Igbo communities with no centralized government had to create warrant chiefs to make the policy work (Afigbo, *Warrant Chiefs*).[1] This necessity forced a transformation on Igbo society, while leaving the monarchical system of most neighboring societies intact, except for the loss of the actual political power of traditional African rulers. *"Pacification,"* in the last sentence of the novel, meant imposing the supreme authority of the British government on all African societies whether or not they had monarchs or centralized governments. The "pacification" of Igbo territory was a troublesome affair. Since the Igbo had no overall government, it meant the separate conquest of each Igbo community, "Umuofia" as well as "Abame." The British approach to administration did not, in the long run, inhibit the preservation of ethnic variety. But it began the process of change: the old judicial system declined; the ancestral spirits, awesome judges, and the spirits that presided at important religious and social ceremonies were subsequently reduced to mere entertainers on Christian feast days; the highest political title of king, *eze*, reemerged, and its holders began to claim a higher social status than they had previously.

All the different European approaches to colonial rule achieved the single historical purpose of transforming traditional African communities into members of the worldwide community created by the expansion of modern European capitalism. Clearly then, a study of Achebe's novel should focus on two important issues: first, the urgent need to change the existing perception of things African, and second, Achebe's re-creation of the Igbo as a distinct African society that has developed a self-sustaining culture, rejecting the monarchical system and traditions of migrations from outside Nigeria. In stressing this view of the Igbo, Achebe recognizes that art can be as much an idealized account of reality as an imaginative record. For him, fiction is not merely something that springs from a poet's imaginings. It is "another way of looking at reality" (Ogbaa, "Interview" 2).

Two myths flourished in the European knowledge of the lower Niger peoples before and during the colonial period Achebe describes. One was that no real difference existed among the ethnic groups in black Africa; the other was that the Igbo people were almost completely isolated from the outside world.

The myth of a common ethnic identity has much truth, especially among the peoples of the southern parts of West Africa. Most of their languages belong to the same family, and their traditional religious beliefs and rituals are similar. The Igbo and their neighbors shared a four-day week whose cycle was closely tied to markets, religious observances, and the system of giving names at birth.[2] Strong similarities also exist in the content and form of festivals, ceremonies, sports, and kinship ties. The new yam festival, which brings the agricultural cycle to a climax, celebrates a crop that is economically and ceremonially important in the savannah and forest regions of West Africa. The kola nut, produced in the forest zone, has very much the same ritual and nutritional uses throughout the region.

The myth of Igbo isolation arose, in part, because the Igbo inhabit a forest homeland in small village communities. While this settlement pattern is not unique to the Igbo, it is not typical in other areas of either the savannah or the forest belt of West Africa. In these other areas traditional urban centers served as seats of international commerce and of the many empires that flourished in the region at various times in the last one thousand years. Although Achebe's artistic intention turns on this key difference, he does not suggest that the Igbo never experienced this other form of political organization. Turning away from that complex history, Achebe deliberately underpins his fictional account with the theory held by many Igbo thinkers, that the republican form of organization "evolved" from the kind of religious monarchy that once flourished at Nri. From this different Igbo ethos, Achebe creates the motivation behind the actions of Okonkwo, the hero who aspires toward the highest title in the land. The Igbo do not have ascribed or inherited titles that Okonkwo is not permitted to seek.

In focusing on a specific period of recent Igbo history, Achebe avoids historical material that would have given instant prestige to his subject. African historians of the late 1950s and early 1960s emphasized African empires of the past to enhance the status of African history. This conception of African history dominated the whole succeeding decade. Thus, in reviewing a book on the archaeological discoveries at Igbo-Ukwu sites at Nri, A. E. Afigbo argued that it was "probably through the corridors of Nri history that the Igbo will come to occupy their proper place in the majestic story of the rise of Negro civilization" ("On the Threshold" 216).

Because this model of African historiography prevailed as Achebe was writing his novel, he could have opted for a majestic story and produced a historical novel on Nri hegemony, drawing on the studies of ethnographers like Leonard and Basden, whose works he knew, for supplementary material. As Robert M. Wren points out, "Achebe never mentions [Nri], yet his own ancestral clan traces its descent from Nri" (*Achebe's World* 78). At a time when many other Nigerian peoples were explaining their origins in terms of migrations or cultural links with prestigious civilizations, Achebe did not even look as far as Nri. The story he tells begins at Umuofia. Achebe's strategy seems to reflect a fundamental Igbo attitude of individualism and independence in a fairly accurate manner. Elizabeth Isichei quotes an Igbo elder as saying, "[W]e did not come from anywhere, and anyone who tells you we came from anywhere is a liar. Write it down" (*History* 3). Nri, considered by many as "the fountain-head from which all the other clans have sprung" (Leonard 35), represents high culture, with its priestly hegemony and rich material culture. Achebe's preference for a different concept of homeland is seen in his choice of *Umuofia* as the name of his fictional clan. The prefix *Umu-* means "children of" or "descendants of," and *-ofia* means "bush" or "wilderness," indicating the name of either the clan's eponymous ancestor or the community's forest setting.[3]

Achebe compares Okonkwo's first, sensational victory as a wrestler with the fight in which "the founder of their town engaged a spirit of the wild for seven days and seven nights" (3). Thus, in the very first paragraph, Achebe strikes two key themes of the novel, the taming of the wild and the courage and strength required to dominate and control the environment. Umuofia celebrates these qualities through its wrestling festivals, its wars (with their mementos of human heads), and its yam festivals (*Ahajioku*), for the yam culture is a direct product of the taming of the forest (Isichei, *History* 7; Afigbo, *Ropes* 125). Umuofia has gone down in local history as *obodo dike*, the land of the brave, even though this ethos becomes too difficult for Unoka and his son Okonkwo who, ironically, has inherited the abilities of the town's mythical founder. Achebe presents the heroic action on a scale that is appropriate to the character of Umuofia. Even though Okonkwo reinforces his "incredible prowess in two inter-tribal wars" by collecting his fifth human head in the latest war (6), his achievement does not fully suggest the scale of the wars and the bloodshed that were taking place elsewhere in the nineteenth century, among groups to the north, west, and east of the Igbo, decades before these groups suffered pacification at the hands of the British. The wars of Umuofia are wars between related clans, not wars of conquest and territorial expansion.

By controlling the scale of the novel's action, Achebe affirms the myth of Igbo isolation from the rest of the world. Of course, Umuofia is not isolated from other Igbo villages. The text indicates that virtually all the other Igbo clans are involved in Umuofia's activities and are thereby included in the circle of relative seclusion, interacting with one another through markets, festivals, rituals, and wars. At a celebration of the earth goddess soon after the introduction of Christianity into Umuofia, "all the masked *egwugwu* of Umuofia . . . came from all the . . . neighbouring villages. . . . from Imo, . . . from Uli" (132). The Imo River flows through the heart of eastern Igbo country, down to its southern limits. The Imo's counterpart in the Northwest is the Anambra River, which flows just east of the Niger River and separates the Igbo from most of their western cousins, whose social institutions— monarchical rather than republican—resemble those of the Edo farther west. Achebe's reference to the Imo thus suggests that the action of the novel covers nearly the entire Igbo country and that Umuofia is an archetype of the Igbo village. The novel's first paragraph reports that the exploits of Amalinze the Cat were known "from Umuofia to Mbaino" (3; *Mbaino* is, literally, *Mba* 'clan' and *ino* 'four'). Achebe uses the structure of Igbo place names to indicate that Amalinze's reputation extended over a fabulous Igbo country. While *Umuofia* connotes the historical depth and autochthony of the Igbo presence at Umuofia through allusion to Igbo myths of origin (as distinct from the legends of migration found among their neighbors), *Mbaino* 'the four clans' hints at the kinship pattern determining the cultural organization and settlement patterns among the Igbo.

The myth of Igbo isolation seems to have originated with the British. Colonial administrators and missionaries often stated that the Igbo people "had little intercourse with the outside world" before the twentieth century (Basden 125). In contrast to this claim, however, is evidence that an eighteenth-century best-seller by Olaudah Equiano, a freed slave, brought some knowledge of the Igbo to the English-speaking reading public (Edwards viii, xviii). Moreover, the Igbo must have imported copper from outside sources, as far back as the ninth century, for making the bronze ornaments that were excavated at Igbo-Ukwu (Shaw, *Unearthing* 72.)

In the late 1950s, when Achebe was writing *Things Fall Apart*, much had been written about African history yet comparatively little had been done for Igbo history.[4] European writers interpreted what was known of African history mainly in the context of European ideas of progress and civilization. They viewed African political systems based on centralized authority as stages of growth, with Western civilization as the norm. Furthermore, they suggested that these institutions had been influenced by the cultures of the Middle East, because they did not credit Africans with the ability to create their own institutions. Achebe had adequate historical material from which he could have developed a case for the existence of a rich material civilization in Africa. He chose instead a different interpretation and told the story of the Igbo people evolving their own humanistic civilization in their relatively secluded forest home.

NOTES

[1]The policy of indirect rule by which the British governed Nigeria was implemented by the governor general, who was based in the capital, Lagos, and who was assisted by three regional governors. The governors, in turn, were assisted by residents and district commissioners, who ruled through local chiefs. Since there was hardly any political hierarchy of paramount chiefs through whom the British could govern Igboland, they issued warrants to appoint as chiefs those persons through whom they wished to govern.

[2]The four Igbo market days were named *Eke, Oye, Afo,* and *Nkwo.* The Igbo derived names from these market days by adding masculine or feminine prefixes (*Nwa-* 'child of,' used for both sexes; masculine: *Oko-* 'man of'; feminine: *Mgba-* 'woman of'). Examples of such names in *Things Fall Apart* are Okonkwo, Okafo, Nwafo, Mgbafo, Okoye, Nwoye.

[3]Afigbo reports a suggestion that the term *Igbo* at first meant "the people of the bush" (*Ropes* 40). No other evidence has turned up to support this definition. But among the Yoruba, with whom the Igbo have some linguistic affinity, a similar term occurs as a descriptive tag in one or two place names such as Ijebu Igbo 'the Ijebu of the bush,' as distinct from the Ijebu of the town, for example.

[4]The argument by some English academic historians that Africa had no history because darkness was not a subject of history caused much indignation among African

scholars and politicians, in the light of the many history books already published about the African past. R. N. Hall's *Great Zimbabwe* (1905), E. W. Bovill's *Caravans of the Old Sahara* (1933), and Basil Davidson's *Old Africa Rediscovered* (1959) are representative of historical scholarship by Europeans. Spanning the period between the beginning of colonialism and the independence of African states, these works provided enough material to suggest the existence of African civilization along the European model.

TEACHING TEXTURE

The Politics of Point of View: Teaching *Things Fall Apart*

Ashton Nichols

Chinua Achebe's *Things Fall Apart* is one of the most teachable texts I have used in the undergraduate classroom. The pedagogical value of the novel stems not only from its status as a classic of modern African literature but also from its stylistic sophistication and its analysis of sociocultural forces in a literary context. Achebe's direct prose style combines with the novel's richness of detail and powerful emotions to produce a text that is easily accessible to a wide range of undergraduate students. At the same time, *Things Fall Apart* challenges a whole series of common assumptions about perspective and cultural relativity in fiction. As a novel, the text provides numerous opportunities for an analysis of genre, authorial point of view, narrative organization, and the use of dialogue. As a work of literature, *Things Fall Apart* widens narrow literary concerns by addressing a variety of historical and cultural questions about the relations among races, between the "civilized" and the "primitive" world, and between cultures in conflict from within and without.

I have included the novel in freshman honors courses and in special-topics classes organized around themes such as The Colonial Mind and Colonizing Consciousness. In these courses, students read Achebe in conjunction with other works that offer a multicultural perspective: Rudyard Kipling's *Kim*, Joseph Conrad's *Heart of Darkness*, E. M. Forster's *Passage to India*, Ngugi wa Thiong'o's *Weep Not, Child*. I also use the novel in a course entitled The Literature of Colonization, in which I include additional works by Jean

Rhys, Okot p'Bitek, Derek Walcott, and Buchi Emecheta. In all these classes, I introduce *Things Fall Apart* as an early narrative of colonization from the point of view of the colonized peoples. This organization allows students to place the novel in a historical perspective, as well as to begin their reading of Achebe with a set of expectations raised by the colonizers: Kipling, Conrad, and Forster. Since the locus of meaning and the level of irony vary widely among these colonial writers, students are already prepared for the fluctuations in interpretation that characterize works involving a plurality of perspectives.

I do not give a background lecture to *Things Fall Apart*. By reading the first eight chapters without any specific preparatory information, students find themselves immediately dropped into a world that seems very foreign. As a result they are forced to generate their own point of view, a stance from which they analyze and interpret the text. I begin the first class with a series of questions designed to focus attention on the ways individual students arrived at their particular vantage points: Did you identify with Okonkwo? Did you sympathize with him? Who are the sympathetic characters in the village? Does Unoka deserve the censure he receives from his son? Such questions help make this alien world seem less remote. Of course, many works of English literature—from *Beowulf* to *The Waste Land*—may seem more or less culturally alien to middle-class undergraduates in the last decade of the twentieth century. Students respond immediately and enthusiastically, however, to the disjunctions and continuities of Achebe's Igbo world of the lower Niger in the early twentieth century.

One of my students began our first discussion of *Things Fall Apart* by pointing out that she had not realized until she completed the reading assignment that she was identifying with a group of people for whom the white race was still a myth. The first mention of the white race in the novel occurs when Obierika responds to Okonkwo's claim that "[t]he world is large" by saying, "It is like the story of white men who, they say, are white like this piece of chalk. . . . And these white men, they say, have no toes" (51–52). The repeated "they say" is significant at this point; it suggests that accounts of events are often more significant than events themselves. One's beliefs, opinions, and ideas about the world are a function of what one has heard, seen, or been told. Obierika's brother says, "[W]hat is good in one place is bad in another place" (51). This claim, which carries the issue of relativity of judgment into the moral sphere, provides a gloss on the way students enter Achebe's text. Before they have read very far in *Things Fall Apart*, undergraduates realize that their point of view in interpreting the text determines their response to the characters and events.

As a result, class discussion of the novel tends to emphasize the varying perspectives represented within the seemingly integrated Igbo tribe, as well as the conflict between viewpoints that intensifies after the arrival of the white missionaries and settlers. Our first discussion often centers on the details of difference that separate Nigerian village culture from the world inhabited by suburban American undergraduates. The early chapters of the novel are filled with details that demand definition or explication: *jigida* (waist beads), *uli* (dye for skin painting), *ozo* (a rank or title), *ekwe* (wooden drum), *obi* (male living quarters), *chi* (personal god), palm-wine tapping, the kola-nut ceremony, the Evil Forest, titles, bride price, polygamy. Students are impressed at how many of these details Achebe is able to explain in terms of their context. Achebe's decision to retain a number of Igbo words and phrases also generates discussion. What kinds of words does he leave in the original language? Which Igbo words and concepts does he want to translate? The Igbo word *chi*, for example, an individual's personal god, has clear connections to Western concepts of destiny, fate, and the guardian angel; yet, by remaining untranslated, the word retains a sense of its uniquely African meaning. The cumulative effect of the cultural contrasts in the early part of the novel is that students begin moving toward a more open-minded, objectified view of Igbo culture.

At the same time, however, students also want to draw more subjective parallels between Okonkwo's world and Western culture. They point out, for example, the similarities between the oracle Agbala and the oracles of ancient Greece. One of my freshmen noted that the words used to describe the Igbo oracle might have been used to describe its counterpart at Delphi:

> [P]eople came from far and near to consult it. They came when misfortune dogged their steps or when they had a dispute with their neighbours. They came to discover what the future held for them or to consult the spirits of their departed fathers. . . . No one had ever beheld Agbala, except his priestess.   (12)

Students are also quick to notice similarities between the Igbo view of the human condition and traditional Western ideas about tragedy and suffering. Uchendu says, "Do you know how many children I have buried—children I begot in my youth and strength? Twenty-two. I did not hang myself, and I am still alive" (95). One student suggested that Uchendu's speech "sounds like something you would find in Shakespeare." Two of my classes directly connected the Igbo idea of suffering with Greek tragedy. Obierika, for example, mourns Okonkwo's calamity, wondering, "Why should a man suffer so grievously for an offence he had committed inadvertently? But although he thought for a long time he found no answer" (87). When I read aloud Obierika's chastisement of Okonkwo—"What you have done will not please the Earth. It is the kind of action for which the goddess wipes out whole families" (46)—one well-read student said that the image reminded her of the house of Atreus.

Once we have discussed such parallels, we talk about the dangers of universalizing human experience on the basis of apparent similarities. The central conflicts of the novel—the contrast between Okonkwo's masculine heroic tradition and the weakness of his times and the contrast between Umuofia before and after the arrival of the whites—both derive from the impossibility of completely imagining one individual or culture in terms of another. Okonkwo's inability to appreciate the life of his father or his son, like the white colonizer's inability to appreciate that which is valuable in Igbo culture, leads to a series of finally unresolvable conflicts. Achebe is particularly effective at elaborating the problem of perspective. For all its tendency to romanticize tribal life, *Things Fall Apart* does not present a nostalgic picture of traditional society. The Igbo culture leaves infant twins in the Evil Forest to die, sanctions violence as an integral part of life, treats women as possessions, and completely ostracizes the weak and abnormal.

Students soon realize that Achebe is providing a subtle critique of the politics of point of view. Igbo society, in spite of all its positive aspects, is nevertheless susceptible to colonization, at least in part because the Western power structure has a legitimate appeal to many of the villagers. But Achebe also offers a valid critique of all power relations by depicting the forms of exploitation that develop as the missionaries and settlers begin to overwhelm the villagers with a new ideology. According to *Things Fall Apart*, power relations develop in precolonial and colonial Nigeria because certain individuals have a great deal to gain or lose from particular social orderings. Students find rich material for discussion not only in the conflicting perspectives—rigid versus flexible—that characterize Igbo communal society but also in the sequential progression of religion, justice, and education that allows the Europeans such relatively easy ingress into a seemingly stable society.

Teachers can use many of these same issues in *Things Fall Apart* to generate essay topics and exam questions. They can ask students to analyze Okonkwo's character or to describe the conflict between Okonkwo and his own people or between the Igbo villagers and the colonizers. Each of these questions demands close attention to the locus of particular points of view. Teachers can further develop this emphasis by asking students to analyze Okonkwo from the point of view of Nwoye, Obierika, Reverend James Smith, Mr. Brown, or the District Commissioner; from Okonkwo's viewpoint; or from the students' own perspective. Okonkwo becomes a very different character with each shift in perspective. Another effective assignment asks the students to write a draft of the first chapter of the District Commissioner's anticipated volume, *The Pacification of the Primitive Tribes of the Lower Niger*. Later they retell these same events from the standpoint of one or more of the Igbo villagers. Such assignments create a useful framework for interpreting the developing clash of values and cultures. My students often start out wanting to blur the distinctions between Igbo and Western life but then move toward a view that accepts and appreciates difference. At the beginning they try to find Western parallels for every aspect of life in Umuofia, but they end up deciding that Nigerian village culture does not exist to be subsumed under a Westernized set of values and assumptions.

In my classes student essays on *Things Fall Apart* tend to focus on point of view even when the assignment does not call for such an emphasis. One student drew the following conclusion from a character analysis of Okonkwo:

> The conflicting cultures mean a loss of the security and stability Umuofia once had, and this conflict proves to be the source of Okonkwo's downfall.

Another student described the arrival of Christianity in terms of conflicting points of view:

> The central conflict, however, begins with the arrival of Christian missionaries, who violate the pagan gods and divide the society. The Christians are not destroyed for their insane words or for building their church in the Evil Forest. They gain many converts, including Nwoye, Okonkwo's son. Thus, even the family that Okonkwo has fashioned begins to decay.

A third student commented that Nwoye's dual perspective is central to Achebe's purposes in the novel:

> Nwoye's conversion is a good example of how people were generally converted. He is slowly seduced until he feels that his gods won't take revenge for his conversion.

The same student connected point of view with economic well-being, arguing that

> many of the people of Umuofia supported the white intervention. They were won over by the trade items that white people brought. Money flowed into the Igbo economy.

Each of these students has clearly intuited a part of Achebe's thesis: an individual's attitude toward change and tradition is always a function of that individual's place in existing power relations.

The overall effect of teaching *Things Fall Apart* by examining shifting and multiple points of view is that students begin to question and critique their assumptions about cultures and about literature. Such a technique is, of course, not uniquely applicable to this text, but Achebe's novel is particularly useful for analyzing the role of perspective in determining value and meaning. While it may be overly optimistic to suggest that Achebe's narrative allows American students to see through new eyes, *Things Fall Apart* does demand that readers widen their perspectives. Achebe also raises interesting questions about the social role of literature and our judgments of literary merit. The novel expands the concerns of much modernist and postmodernist fiction by suggesting that literature still has a vital cultural role to play as we near the end of the twentieth century. A number of my students have gone on to read other colonial and postcolonial works as a result of their exposure to Achebe.

As teachers, we should rethink our ways of approaching all literary texts. Achebe's novels (not just *Things Fall Apart*), like works by Ngugi, Emecheta, p'Bitek, George Lamming, Wole Soyinka, and others, should find their way into our courses. Such texts are valuable not only because they expand the canon of teachable texts—in fact, we should guard against "colonizing" these works for literature courses—but also because they teach us about the process of reading. By forcing us to acknowledge the relation between the reader's point of view and conflicting interpretations, Achebe suggests one way that meaning emerges in all literary texts. Like our students, we need to remember that meaning is the result not so much of what we read as of who we imagine ourselves to be while we are reading.

A wide range of literary concerns are thus accessible through *Things Fall Apart*: questions of narrative structure, the analysis of genre, the role of dialogue and description, the function of the narrator. But *Things Fall Apart*, like much of the postcolonial literature that has followed it, expands the narrowly literary to include a much wider range of social and political issues: How can individuals treat one another more justly in existing societies? When do the rights of one cultural or religious group infringe on the rights of another? What is the relation between ideology and power in societies torn by conflict among cultures? To what extent does a person's point of view determine that individual's relation to society? In teaching *Things Fall Apart* through the politics of point of view, I have found that Achebe's novel appeals to students not only as individuals interested in literature but as members of the human community.

The Paradoxical Characterization of Okonkwo

Arlene A. Elder

Why does Okonkwo end tragically? This question haunts every reader of *Things Fall Apart*, for we sense that a satisfactory answer would explain not only Chinua Achebe's complex protagonist but also the writer's larger concern about the destruction of traditional African society during the period of colonization. Students used to typical Western protagonists struggle to classify Okonkwo as either a hero or an antihero and to discover the tragic flaw that leads to his defeat. Through a sensitive reading of the novel and an introduction to Achebe's critical judgment of his hero, an instructor can help students detect the writer's ambivalence both toward Igbo society at the time of colonial contact and toward Christianity and the British governmental structures. A fruitful way to analyze Okonkwo, therefore, is to have students determine, through internal and external evidence, how easily he fits into the Igbo community, whether he exemplifies its values, and why he takes an isolated stand against the colonizers. Such an examination reveals a paradoxical protagonist who, by his people's judgment and his own, is a trustworthy representative of the traditions of his clan but whose individualism finally leads to his defeat.

Things Fall Apart spans the volatile transition period when British missionaries and colonial officials were making rapid inroads into western Nigeria. Achebe's refusal to place blame for the destruction of Igbo society completely on the West provides students with a context for the historical events depicted in his work. In response to the question, "Who do you really blame?" Achebe replies:

> [T]he coming of the missionaries is very complex, and I cannot simply assign blame to this man or that man. The society itself was already heading toward destruction . . . [but] Europe has a lot of blame. . . . [T]here were internal problems that made it possible for the Europeans to come in. Somebody showed them the way. A conflict between two brothers enables a stranger to reap their harvest.   (Egejuru 125)

This dual view of the causes of colonial destruction provides some of the most interesting tensions in Achebe's books. Moreover, in *Things Fall Apart*, Okonkwo, characterized both as a typical Igbo man and as an individualist acting in a very complicated way in and on his community, is a microcosm of the conflicting energies in Igboland, catalyzed by the antagonistic intrusion of the Europeans.

One possible explanation for Achebe's duality in assigning historical guilt is his own dual African and Western background. He has called *Things Fall Apart* "an act of atonement with my past, the ritual return and homage of a prodigal son" (*Morning* 70). This statement indicates his intention to educate Nigerian readers about their traditions and reveals, in its biblical allusion, his grounding in Christianity. Achebe's father was a church teacher, and his grandfather welcomed the first missionaries to his village of Ogidi. "All this is part of my inheritance," Achebe realizes, "and I try to interpret all of it" (Egejuru 80). Like his creator, Okonkwo is a man of dualities; his tensions, however, can best be understood as social and psychological rather than historical.

The first step in examining Okonkwo as both a typical Igbo man and an individualist is to determine which basic Igbo qualities he demonstrates. Moving from general cultural considerations to a specific examination of character is a useful and appropriate approach to all novels, especially African works like *Things Fall Apart* whose historical background may not be well known to Western students.

Although we recognize the day-by-day unity of Igbo traditional life, for purposes of analysis we can classify the clan's characteristics as occupational, social, and spiritual, and, in every instance, Okonkwo seems the perfect expression of them. Achebe pictures the Igbo as an agricultural people who prosper through hard work. Okonkwo, when we first meet him, is a farmer, wealthy enough to have taken a third wife, happiest when he is laboring on his land. Physical strength is honored among these people, and Achebe's hero—"tall and huge" (3)—has won fame not only as the greatest wrestler in the nine villages but as a great warrior in intertribal conflicts, having brought home five heads. Achebe's use of proverbial language enhances the richness of *Things Fall Apart*, and the author points out that "[a]mong the Ibo the art of conversation is regarded very highly, and proverbs are the palm-oil with which words are eaten" (5). At first, his protagonist strikes us as too much the man of action, too impatient, to share this linguistic facility with his people, but a closer reading reveals that even the laconic Okonkwo occasionally delights in the Igbo love of language. To justify the elaborate feast he gives as a farewell to his mother's people after his exile, he explains, with a well-known saying, "I cannot live on the bank of a river and wash my hands with spittle" (117).

Moreover, Okonkwo achieves success among his people by earning two titles and being chosen to become an *egwugwu*, a representative of one of the clan's ancestors. "Age was respected among his people," we are told, "but achievement was revered"; Okonkwo's "fame rested on solid personal achievements" (3, 6). His great passion is "to become one of the lords of the clan. That had been his life-spring" (92). Even toward the end, in a passage subtly indicating a disruption of Igbo cohesiveness, Okonkwo is praised as an upholder of the traditions. One of the oldest residents of Mbanta congratulates him by noting, "It is good in these days when the younger generation consider themselves wiser than their sires to see a man doing things in the grand, old way" (118).

Nevertheless, despite Okonkwo's adherence to tradition and his honor in the clan, his life is filled with sometimes inexplicable misfortunes, most significantly his accidental killing of Ezeudu's son, which lead to his seven-year exile from Umuofia. Like Obierika, his closest friend, we feel compelled to make sense of such bad luck to better understand the meaning of not only Okonkwo's life but life in general. To do so, we must again contextualize, this time recalling Igbo metaphysics, specifically the concept of a personal god, or *chi*. Ruminating over what has happened to him, Okonkwo laments:

> Clearly his . . . *chi* was not made for great things. A man could not rise beyond the destiny of his *chi*. The saying of the elders was not true—that if a man said yea his *chi* also affirmed. Here was a man whose *chi* said nay despite his own affirmation. (92)

We recognize Okonkwo's conclusion here as evidence of his depression and self-pity rather than as a valid criticism of Igbo teaching, which admits, "a man may struggle with all his power and say yes most emphatically and yet nothing he attempts will succeed" (*Morning* 97).

Understandably self-absorbed after his banishment, Okonkwo forgets his people's complex perception of the mysterious struggle between destiny and the individual will. The Igbo live with the paradox inherent in this metaphysical problem, but Okonkwo fastens onto an interpretation that makes him feel the most powerful and the most unfairly treated. His continuing self-pity in Mbanta evokes a telling rebuke from his uncle, Uchendu, who warns against a kind of negative individualism:

> You think you are the greatest sufferer in the world. . . . Have you not heard the song they sing when a woman dies?
> "For whom is it well, for whom is it well?
> There is no one for whom it is well." (95)

To help students understand Okonkwo's character, which troubles them from the beginning, and to clarify Achebe's intentions, the instructor needs to leave contexts, for a moment, as resonating forces in the background and concentrate on the protagonist as an individual. Among the Igbo, we must remember, "a man was judged according to his own worth and not according to the worth of his father" (6). Yet Okonkwo is a man "possessed by the fear of his father's contemptible life and shameful death" (13). He is "ruled by one passion—to hate everything that his father Unoka had loved. One of those things was gentleness and another was idleness" (10). His fear of idleness leads to his productivity, and his fear of gentleness leads to a brusqueness with less successful men—"Okonkwo knew how to kill a man's spirit"—and to a domination of his household, which he rules "with a heavy hand" (9, 19). The subordination of women to men in the Igbo social system is not unique to Okonkwo's compound, of course. The novel offers us the general wisdom, "No matter how prosperous a man was, if he was unable to rule his women and his children (and especially his women) he was not really a man" (37).

As we focus on the protagonist, however, it becomes obvious that we must continually relate our interpretation of his ideas and actions to the values of his society. For instance, we begin to suspect that Okonkwo's harsh, tyrannical nature signifies more than a simple attempt to make him appear unsympathetic and overbearing when, in a rage, he violates a taboo by beating his youngest wife during the Week of Peace. The high priest warns him, " 'The evil you have done can ruin the whole clan.' . . . And so people said he had no respect for the gods of the clan" (22). In settling another household's domestic dispute, Evil Forest, who speaks for the *egwugwu*, declares, "It is not bravery when a man fights with a woman" (66). This judgment of the ancestors on an action like Okonkwo's indicates that, although Okonkwo is an *egwugwu* himself, his insecurity and bad temper frequently lead him to act contrary to his society's values, even to the extent of endangering his people. His subsequent killing of Ikemefuna, a heart-rending result of precisely the same weakness and an act readers find more horrible than the prior wife-beating, is actually not as serious because, in this instance, Okonkwo has chosen (questionably, it is true) to participate in the judgment of the clan.

The individualism that leads Okonkwo to profane the Week of Peace becomes a key factor in his characterization, and his refusal to be guided by the clan's traditions and wishes becomes most significant in the third part of the novel. After he returns to Umuofia he finds that, since the advent of the white settlers, "[t]he clan had undergone such profound change . . . that it was barely recognizable" (129). At this point, ironically, Okonkwo's symbolic link to his people shows most clearly. His personal misfortune at the end of part 1 seems a harbinger of the decline of all the Igbo. Like Okonkwo, his clan seems unfairly visited by ill fortune since it adheres to the ancient religious and social codes that supposedly guarantee protection by the gods. Yet, the white colonists come and remain, an inexorable force, promising the destruction of these very gods. Teachers should point out this prophetic aspect of Achebe's hero as a typical Igbo, since it complicates the themes of social representativeness and personal individualism noted earlier.

From the start, Okonkwo urges violence against the missionaries. His view, it is true, resembles that of traditional figures like Chielo, the priestess of Agbala, who "called the converts the excrement of the clan" (101). Okonkwo disagrees with the majority, however, who believe the gods can defend themselves, and, significantly, with the growing number of ordinary people in Umuofia, who enjoy the wealth the colonists' trading store brings and who listen to the missionaries' arguments about the practicality of educating Igbo children.

That his unyielding rejection of the whites links him to an ever-weakening past is not initially clear to Okonkwo. When he successfully convinces the clan to use violent retribution to revenge Enoch's unmasking of an *egwugwu*, "[i]t was like the good old days again, when a warrior was a warrior" (136). But Obierika's prophetic warning, "It is already too late," becomes vividly true when the henchmen of the District Commissioner punish Okonkwo and the other clan leaders (124). Personally humiliated, Okonkwo resolves, in a characteristic desire to reclaim power, to take individual action against the whites if necessary: "If Umuofia decided on war, all would be well. But if they chose to be cowards he would go out and avenge himself" (141). His nostalgic thoughts, "Worthy men are no more. . . . Those were days when men were men," suggest his anachronistic, isolated position as surely as the incongruity of his raffia war dress (141).

Okonkwo realizes that Umuofia will not go to war. He murders the court messenger in an individualistic act not at all representative of the wishes of his people—"He heard voices asking: 'Why did he do it?' " (145)—and one guaranteed to bring down the wrath of the colonial administration on Umuofia, as it had come down on Abame, which was no more.

Okonkwo's subsequent suicide strikes us as both terrifying and richly ambiguous. By such an act, he ironically brings on himself a shameful death like his father's, a fate he has expended tremendous energy all his life to avoid. Achebe leaves us asking why Okonkwo engages in irrevocable self-destruction that contradicts everything he has lived for. This problem offers a splendid opportunity for students to examine Achebe's use of ambiguity. One explanation of the suicide could be that Okonkwo recognizes, finally, that he is a man out of time. His values no longer resemble those of his society; therefore, no honorable life remains for him. Another possibility is that since a proud man would be galled at the inevitable capture and punishment by the despised whites, his death cheats them of their revenge. Of course, he may also intend his suicide as a mocking commentary on what he perceives as the present, debased values of his clan. Although the Igbo have abandoned the standards of their fathers, Okonkwo's self-murder might provide a "shock of recognition" that forces them not only to realize that at least one of their traditions—the refusal to touch the bodies of suicides—is still operative but also to confront the inconsistency of their position. Possibly, the suicide is simply a contemptuous "pox on both their houses." Some students may suggest that suicide is madness and that, by the end, Okonkwo is not thinking rationally at all; his death merely reflects his mental and emotional destruction.

Whatever Okonkwo's final violent act signifies—that he recognizes his failure, that he knowingly condemns his people and the colonizers, or that he is, ultimately, mad and personally meaningless—his motivation is finally beside the point. His suicide represents an individualistic response that ironically coincides with the flaws Achebe considers responsible for the rapid inroads made by colonialism. Uchendu, the elder of Mbanta who advocates traditional ways, believes that the encroachment of the Christians results from the weakening of kinship ties among the younger generation: "[Y]ou do not understand how strong is the bond of kinship. You do not know what it is to speak with one voice. And what is the result? An abominable religion has settled among you" (118). Achebe has observed that the

> concept of the worth of the individual is always limited by another concept, the concept of the voice of the community. For instance, Okonkwo's extreme individualism leads to working against the will of the people and to self-destruction. And anybody who wanders off beyond what is accepted as appropriate for the individual, or a person who sets himself in opposition, quite often is heading for destruction.
> (Egejuru 123)

Achebe recognizes, however, that strong individuals like Okonkwo often cause a society to analyze its generally accepted views. After the ritual slaughter of Ikemefuna, such analysis occurs when Obierika ponders the unquestioned destruction of innocents. He wonders about his acceptance of the decree to "throw away" twins, whom the Igbo consider an abomination to the earth. As Achebe notes, "At least some questioning of the system is taking place and that is because a man has held up the values of the society to itself and sort of said, 'This is what you say you approve of. Do you really approve or not?' " (Egejuru 124).

Despite his appreciation of such challenges to established practices, however, Achebe, finally, is not ambivalent about Okonkwo's actions: "no man," he says, "can be greater or wiser than his community no matter how important he is" (Egejuru 126). As the protagonist in *Things Fall Apart*, Okonkwo does not function as a singular hero or antihero, arousing love or hatred; instead, he is a figure deliberately designed to raise the very questions readers are prompted to ask: "What did he stand for? What was the destruction about? What are the echoes that are left in the society?" (Egejuru 129). The paradoxical treatment of Okonkwo reflects not only the author's interest in the protagonist's psychological complexity but also a concern about the fragmenting danger of individualism, a flaw that Achebe sees as responsible, at least partially, for the devastation of colonialism. "That man was one of the greatest men in Umuofia . . . ," laments Obierika, "and now he will be buried like a dog" (147). To help students account for this apparent injustice, teachers should encourage them not to concentrate exclusively on the frequently contradictory personal qualities of Okonkwo—his insecurity as opposed to his arrogance, for instance. Students should also avoid focusing on the irony of the decline in Okonkwo's personal fortune as well as on their response of liking or disliking him. Instead they should recognize his larger symbolic function in the novel as representative of the suicidal fragmentation of Igbo society.

TRADITIONAL PARADIGMS AND MODERN INTERTEXTUALITY

Matrical Approach to *Things Fall Apart*: A Poetics of Epic and Mythic Paradigms

Ousseynou B. Traoré

Chinua Achebe's *Things Fall Apart* is widely taught in universities throughout the world. In the American context, the novel commonly appears in the history, sociology, political science, world civilizations, and literature curricula. In the 1990s, as the canon expands to include non-Western texts and gender studies, the teaching of *Things Fall Apart* in English and comparative literature courses poses serious problems of tradition, narrative theory, critical approach, and pedagogy. In what tradition does the novel belong? How does this tradition affect a theoretical account of its form? What analytical approach best opens the "closed" areas of the text, extends its surface meanings, and maximizes the students' enlightened enjoyment? How do we teach this African classic in scholarly infrastructures that remain essentially Eurocentric, when we even cross-list African literature or black studies with English or comparative literature?

From Chaucer to Achebe: Canonical Problems

As I wrote the first draft of this essay in December 1987, I was winding up a three-week discussion of *Things Fall Apart* in an undergraduate course,

English 102: Composition and Literature, at the University of Southwestern Louisiana. I had substituted Achebe's novel for the *Odyssey*, to supplement our major text, the *Heath Guide to Literature*. The *Heath Guide* and Homer's *Odyssey* had been selected by the Freshman Committee, a group of white men and women trained in English and well aware of Western world literatures. The committee had given the instructors the choice of a "modern" novel in lieu of the *Odyssey*, with the assumption that whatever novels the instructors chose would still fall in line, in the same way as the *Odyssey*, with the notions and principles of "literature" generically posited by the *Heath Guide* and other approved textbooks.

Because I teach literature as an ideological practice, my first lecture always covers issues of dominance, culture, economics, race, gender, and ideology under the rubric of the sociology of literary studies. In this context, I address the concepts of literary production and the scholarly infrastructure. I survey the course offerings of the department listed in the catalog and point out the Eurocentric nature of the canon, the larger context that governs our course and the book selections.

Even though the *Heath Guide* contains a few United States minority and Third World texts, these are not placed in their own traditions but are effectively governed by theories and examples of Western literature explicit and implicit in our textbook. The *Heath Guide* contains selections from Boccaccio, Catullus, Homer, Archilochus, Sophocles, Dante, Chaucer, Shakespeare, Milton, Yeats, Conrad, and a fair representation of major modern European and Anglo-American literatures. These selections tend to confirm the average student's assumed view of literature. Over the first twelve weeks, through close reading and critical discussions, we identify major components of Europoetics shared by the Western texts. Throughout this time, at regular intervals, I use the non-Western selections in the *Heath Guide*, contrasting them with the Western ones, to address issues of comparative aesthetics, internal and external colonialism, and autonomous canons; all these issues lead to, and are fully illustrated later by, Achebe's novel, our last item on the semester's reading list.

At first glance, however, the very substitution of *Things Fall Apart* for Homer's classical work might suggest shared and unbroken canonical bloodlines between the African text and the Eurocentric literary matrix of the *Heath Guide*, in which an excerpt of Homer's masterpiece is even reprinted. Indeed, the blurb on the back cover and the "Note about the Title" in the Fawcett Crest–Ballantine paperback edition of Achebe's text make the explicitly Western literary connections the *Heath Guide* prepares us for. The blurb describes the novel as "a classic of modern African writing" and "a powerful and moving narrative that critics have compared with classic Greek tragedy." The note informs us that "[t]he title for Chinua Achebe's first novel, *Things Fall Apart*, is taken from William Butler Yeats' poem, 'The

Second Coming,' " and situates the novel squarely in a Western literary and cultural tradition by quoting Judith Gleason, who argues that *"Things Fall Apart* comes from the world of Yeats' cataclysmic vision, and [that] the Irish poet would have appreciated the wild old Nigerian" (4).

I use the blurb and the note, two major statements that frame our text of Achebe's *Things Fall Apart*, to sensitize the students to the problems of comparative aesthetics and canonization: How can Achebe's novel "come from the world of Yeats' cataclysmic vision" and be a "classic of African writing"? Achebe reports an interesting joke that brilliantly captures the problems of Eurocentric canonical assumptions. "Only fifteen years ago," Achebe writes in a 1973 address, "a bright, skeptical academic at a Nigerian university could raise a laugh by saying: *that would be the day when English literature is taught from Chaucer to Achebe"* ("Thoughts" 54). The *Heath Guide* marks the beginning of English literature with an excerpt from the *Canterbury Tales* and then takes us further back in literary history to Roman and Greek "great books," such as Homer's *Odyssey.*[1]

Teaching and studying *Things Fall Apart* as "a classic of African writing" in an academic structure governed by the "great books" and their descendants leads one to argue, as Charles Nnolim does, that *Things Fall Apart* is "an Igbo National Epic . . . modelled on the celebrated Anglo-Saxon epic, *Beowulf,* although it at the same time shows certain basic affinities with other classical epics like Homer's *Odyssey* and Virgil's *Aeneid"* (55). Nnolim is right about reading or teaching *Things Fall Apart* as an Igbo national epic, but the models of the novel must be located in Igbo and African matrices.

Identifying Matrical Paradigms

Dramatizing the canonical and Eurocentric aesthetic surrounding the teaching or study of *Things Fall Apart* enables me to legitimize an alternative, African-Igbo framework in which to construct our non-Western notion of the classic. I lecture on African oral traditions, providing detailed discussions of several genres, including proverbs, riddles, myths, clan and family histories, and epics. I give examples and summarize the plots of canonized African oral texts such as Djibril T. Niane's *Sundiata,* relating them to the issues of culture, politics, aesthetics, and sociohistorical events. I then talk about Achebe's work, reading relevant excerpts from his published essays on "applied art" and his ideological explorations of the much debated past. Since the choice of tradition and form are ideological and since Achebe's work reflects his colonial experience and his response to specific works by Joyce Cary and Joseph Conrad, as well as to the Eurocentric scholarship he calls "colonialist criticism" (*Morning* 3–18), I read the following passage from his discussion of the *chi* in Igbo cosmology:

> Since Igbo people did not construct a rigid and closely argued system
> of thought to explain the universe and the place of man in it, preferring
> the metaphor of myth and poetry, anyone seeking an insight into their
> world must seek it along their own way. Some of these ways are folk-
> tales, proverbs, proper names, rituals and festivals.   ("Chi" 94)

Now the students' attention is effectively directed away from the worlds
of Yeats and his classical forebears. We enter *Things Fall Apart* through
Achebe's ancestors and "their world." I ask the students to locate and read
aloud the myths, folktales, poetry, and proverbs in the novel, as well as the
passages about festivals and ritual performances. I group these excerpts into
two categories, epic and mythic matrices. Since these matrices inform the
world of *Things Fall Apart* and saturate the novel, the matrical approach is
an excellent tool for exploring formal and thematic issues. This approach
develops a poetics of epic and mythic paradigms that subsumes rituals,
performances, and festivals under what Wole Soyinka calls "primary paradigms," undatable vehicles of self-apprehension and racial-ethnic origins (8).

Theory and Poetics

In class, through the matrical analysis, we attempt to identify the formal
and thematic relations between the myths, proverbs, and tales and the
fictional context in which they are embedded. What specific rules govern
their aesthetic combinations? I suggest that we look at African oral models,
the art of the classical works of oral prose, including Niane's *Sundiata* and
Amos Tutuola's *Palm-Wine Drinkard* (I taught *The Palm-Wine Drinkard* in
my spring 1989 course United States Minority and Third World Literature).
In the foreword to *African Prose I*, Achebe informs us that "the finest
examples of oral prose occur . . . in oratory" and that "the good orator calls
to his aid the legends, folk-lore, proverbs, etc., of his people; they are some
of the raw material with which he works" (vii–viii). We should look to this
vernacular realm for the "classical" and "epic" forebears of Achebe's novel,
the "master[s] in the art of eloquence" who call themselves "the vessels of
speech" (Niane 1).

In *Things Fall Apart* the orator uses the proverbs, tales, and myths to
structure his prose and display its complex philosophical meanings. The
shorter narratives and other forms of oral art found in the text serve as
thematic and structural models for significant fictional events. The parallels
between the paradigms and the fiction modeled after them put in motion a
metaphorical process that binds the written and oral forms in a rich and
complex narrative governed by consistent rules integral to theme, character,
and plot. As a class, we set out to prove this thesis through detailed, close
reading.

Next, I ask the students to list major characters, events, and themes as a basis for discussing the poetics sketched here. Our attention focuses on a significant cast: Okonkwo, Ikemefuna, Ezinma, Ekwefi, the male and female deities Agbala and Ani, respectively, and their female and male human agents. We discern two major themes and their repeatable variations: the crisis of nationalist leadership at the moment of colonial conquest and the suicidal gender imbalance in Okonkwo's character that leads to and explains his death.

As the discussion goes on, I draw diagrams on the board, break down thematically important Igbo names and words, and group images according to the thematic distributions of gender and leadership issues. We notice, for example, that the tale of the tortoise and the birds supplies a complete paradigm for the story of Okonkwo; it contains epic and nonepic models of the symbolic kingship metaphorically associated with Okonkwo. The mythic stories, such as "Mosquito and Ear" and "Why the Snake-lizard Killed His Mother," offer variational paradigms of Okonkwo's gender imbalance and govern his abominable and nonepic acts.

Analytical Model: Eating with Kings

To illustrate a typical class discussion, I conclude this essay with a matrical analysis of an epic paradigm that describes a significant aspect of Okonkwo's character: the fragment of Umuofia's foundation myth embedded in the novel's first paragraph. Following the thematic and structural rules that govern other similar paradigms, this model occurs in a thematically relevant fictional environment and helps the reader apprehend reality through the metaphor of myth. The foundation myth provides a positive epic hero model for Okonkwo and confers the symbolic kingship of the founder on Okonkwo. It links the founding of Umuofia with Okonkwo's arduous personal achievement and rise to national fame as a wrestler at the age of eighteen, the threshold of his adult life:

> Okonkwo threw [Amalinze the Cat] in a fight which the old men agreed was one of the fiercest since the founder of their town engaged a spirit of the wild for seven days and seven nights.   (3)

Through juxtaposition and comparison, the parallel structures of the mythic fragment and Okonkwo's wrestling match establish a metaphorical process that equates Okonkwo's personal deed with the epic act of the founding ancestor. The image of the spirit of the wild, whom the founder engages at the risk of his own safety on behalf of the clan, is reflected in the character of Amalinze, who is called "the Cat because his back would never touch the earth" (3). The metaphor ontologically equates Okonkwo's opponent with the spirit of the wild, magnifying Okonkwo's personal risk as he participates in this reenactment. Further, the duration of the founder's fight, seven days and seven nights, parallels Amalinze's seven years of unchallenged reign as a wrestling king.

The epic proportions of Okonkwo's deeds and the supernatural odds against him are best understood in the light of Soyinka's theory of the "ritual archetype" as primary paradigm. He writes:

> The epic celebrates the victory of the human spirit over forces inimical to self-extension. It concretises in the form of action the arduous birth of the individual or communal entity, creates a new being through the utilizing and stressing of the language of self-glorification. . . . Man can shelve and even overwhelm metaphysical uncertainties by epic feats, and prolong such a state of social euphoria by their constant recital. . . . It required a challenger, a human representative to breach [the realm of infinity] periodically on behalf of the well-being of the community.   (2–3)

The founder's deed marks the birth of the new community of Umuofia, while Okonkwo's reenactment of this feat at the New Yam Festival coincides with his self-extension and the creation of his new identity. Through his ritual participation in this event, Okonkwo appropriates the title of his defeated opponent; in the same way, the founder gains sovereignty over his newly cleared area of the bush that was previously ruled by the spirit of the wild. In acquiring the title of "the Cat," Okonkwo also assumes, through metaphorical transfer, the honorific name "Amalinze." Significantly, the etymology of this name reflects the metaphorical language of myth: *Ama* means "clan, road to family"; *lihi* means "on behalf of"; and *nze/eze* means "dodger, agile, artful wrestler or king."[2] The Amalinze title of chieftaincy is conferred on a person who fights on behalf of the clan, one who represents the ideal of an epic and self-sacrificial hero-king.[3]

The story of the founding father is a subtle version of the Ezenri myth of origin. In the oral tradition, Ezenri is the first mythical King of Igboland. Achebe, in his discussion of the *chi*, clearly refers to Ezenri, "that fascinating priest/king whose spiritual pre-eminence was acknowledged over considerable parts of Igboland" ("Chi" 102). In the original myth, Ezenri creates the kingship and the Igbo calendar and brings yam, which the novel tells us is a "man's crop," "the king of crops," one that "stood for manliness" (16, 23, 24). Thus the original kingship of the founder is associated with yam, the symbol of manhood and earned epic kingship. Through the leadership of Ezenri, Achebe writes, "man ceased wandering in the bush and became a settled agriculturist" ("Chi" 103). Achebe captures this reference in the name of Okonkwo's clan, "Umuofia," which means "children of the bush." In the novelistic reworking of the myth, the founder's victory over the spirit of the wild puts an end to the wandering of Okonkwo's people, who clear the bush and crown yam king. The New Yam Festival and the wrestling matches on the second day of the festival mark the reenactment of these mythohistorical events, the creation of a nation and the emergence of the epic leadership of the ancestral "priest/king."

The wrestling praise song, celebrating the victorious Okafo who is "swept off his feet by his supporters and carried home shoulder high," clearly refers to and validates the "Amalinze" ideal conferred metaphorically on Okonkwo:

> Who will wrestle for our village?
>
> . . . .
>
> Has he thrown a hundred Cats?
>
> . . . .
>
> Then send him word to fight for us.   (36)

Achebe uses an important proverb early in the novel to suggest the metaphorical kingship conferred on Okonkwo years after he threw "the Cat," built "two barns full of yams," and took two titles: "As the elders said, if a child washed his hands he could eat with kings. Okonkwo had clearly washed his hands and so he ate with kings and elders" (6). The metaphorical process directly associates Okonkwo with kingship, emphasizing the cleansing ceremony central to this form of mandated governance.

The principle of ritual or symbolic kingship operates in Okonkwo's mission to Mbaino. Okonkwo, the greatest warrior, wrestler, and yam king, is "chosen by the nine villages [of Umuofia] to carry a message of war to their enemies" (19). The mandate from the nine villages, which were founded by the nine sons of the founder, mythicizes the status of Okonkwo, who emerges as a symbolic figure incorporating the founder's nine sons and the ritual kingship of his ancestor. So great is the enemy's fear of Umuofia that "they treated Okonkwo like a king and brought him a virgin who was given to Udo as a wife, and the lad Ikemefuna" (19–20). Ikemefuna, whose name means "let my strength not become lost" (Shelton 91), symbolizes the military strength of the kingship and "belonged to the clan as a whole" (9). Umuofia mandates Okonkwo's custody of this awesome power, and thus, "Okonkwo was . . . asked on behalf of the clan to look after [Ikemefuna]," in accordance with the Amalinze ideal of the epic hero (9). Ikemefuna's symbolic association with the yam metaphor as Okonkwo's ward is particularly noteworthy. In the three years he spends in Okonkwo's care, Ikemefuna "grew rapidly like a yam tendril in the rainy season, and was full of the sap of life" (37). Yam, the "male crop" and the "king of crops," and

Okonkwo's abominable ritual killing of Ikemefuna are rooted in the crisis of epic kingship, since Ikemefuna ("let my strength not become lost"), as a "yam tendril," symbolizes Okonkwo's significant but fragile manhood and epic leadership.

Ikemefuna's song, *eze elina* ("king don't eat it"), grounded in the eating metaphor of the elders' proverb that legitimizes Okonkwo's status, provides another positive model that Okonkwo does not emulate. The song limits the power of the symbolic kingship embodied by Okonkwo, but he refuses to heed the song's interdiction. This disastrous error, which has its roots in his warped ideal of manhood and seems out of balance with the complementary female principle of life, leads to his suicide, an act clearly inscribed in the Snake-lizard model of the tale told by Ezinma and Ekwefi. The nonepic aspects of Okonkwo's character and his gender conflicts are equally well supported by a matrical analysis of relevant myths and proverbs embedded in the novel.

As we pursue this matrical reading of *Things Fall Apart*, the combination of mythic and fictional forms demonstrated above becomes more clearly governed by a consistent set of thematic and structural rules that constitute the narrative grammar of the novel. These rules are identical to those Achebe has identified in Igbo oratory. Thus, in the periods devoted to *Things Fall Apart*, the class explores the gender imbalance and nonepic structures that govern Okonkwo's character, his deadly conflicts with himself, his people, his *chi*, and the Igbo male and female principles of life.[4] From a matrical standpoint firmly grounded in African aesthetic and philosophical systems —no matter what universal correspondences they might have in world literary culture—we can indeed call *Things Fall Apart* a classic of *African* and *world* literature.

NOTES

[1]Indeed, the Modern Language Association's Approaches to Teaching World Literature series confirms the same trajectory. In his preface to the first volume, Joseph Gibaldi writes, "It seems only fitting that the first volume . . . should be devoted to the first great English poet" (ix). The masterpiece was Chaucer's *Canterbury Tales*. The fourth volume revises the canon to include *Beowulf*, "a somewhat earlier great English poem" (Bessinger and Yeager xi).

[2]A Nigerian graduate student at the University of Wisconsin, Madison, provided this etymology while I was writing my dissertation on Achebe in 1979.

[3]Ifeyinwa Okeke, an Igbo student of mine at the University of Southwestern Louisiana in fall 1987, informed me that "Amalinze" is not a proper name but an

honorific title denoting the chieftaincy. Her mother, who happened to have been visiting from Nigeria at the time, was the source of this information.

⁴I have used the matrical approach to explore the poetics of *Things Fall Apart* in undergraduate courses (Composition and Literature, University of Southwestern Louisiana, fall 1987; Imaginative Literature and United States Minority and Third World Literature, Indiana University of Pennsylvania, fall 1988 and spring 1989) and graduate seminars (Conrad and Achebe—Aesthetic Ideology, Alcorn State University, Lorman, Mississippi, spring 1982; Thematic Reversals—The West and the Rest of Us, Indiana University of Pennsylvania, spring 1990). I have also used this approach in a two-day NEH Faculty Seminar, Global Perspectives on Literature Programs, organized by the Department of Comparative Literature, Montclair State College, New Jersey, in June 1984.

"The Tortoise and the Birds":
Strategies of Resistance in *Things Fall Apart*

Barbara Harlow

In *Things Fall Apart*, the fable of the tortoise and the birds explains "why Tortoise's shell is not smooth" (70). According to the fable, which Ekwefi tells her daughter, Ezinma, while her husband, Okonkwo, reclines after dinner, all the birds are invited to attend a great feast in the sky. When Tortoise sees the birds gaily preparing for the happy occasion, he immediately begins to plot his own participation in the gala. There is a famine at the time, and even Tortoise is hungry. Through his "cunning," his "sweet tongue," and his "volubility," Tortoise persuades the birds to include him in their party and even to provide the feathers for his flight (68, 69). He also convinces the birds that they must each take a new name for the great feast. "Our hosts in the sky," he says, "will expect us to honour this age-old custom" (68). Tortoise, who takes for himself the name *All of you*, again appeals to custom when the host of the meal states that the food has been prepared "for all of you." Tortoise then claims that the "custom here is to serve the spokesman first and the others later" (69).

When Tortoise at last finishes eating the repast, the birds are left with only scraps and bones to pick at. Together they decide to take their revenge and reclaim their feathers from the tortoise. Tortoise, dismayed that he cannot return to earth, sends a message to his wife, requesting that she bring all the soft things out of his house so that he will land safely when he jumps from the sky. The messenger, Parrot, brings a different message, however, and Tortoise lands on "hoes, machetes, spears, guns and even his cannon" (70). The village medicine man sticks the bits and pieces of Tortoise's shell back together, and thus it is no longer smooth.

In the context of *Things Fall Apart*, the traditional fable of the tortoise and the birds represents more than indigenous folk wisdom and its interpretation of the natural phenomena of the village world. Published in 1958 on the eve of Nigerian independence but set in turn-of-the-century West Africa during the early period of British colonization, Achebe's first novel proposes, however provisorily, both an outline for national liberation from colonial domination and a critique of restrictive traditionalism as an alternative to the colonial present. The tortoise's tale, told by Ekwefi, one of Okonkwo's four wives,[1] describes not only the fate of Tortoise after the great feast in the sky but the transformation of Parrot as well. Parrot, stereotypically gullible, obliging, and capable only of repeating someone else's words, becomes an active historical agent who uses language creatively to help himself and the other birds. The tale insists, however, that rhetorical skill alone is not enough, and it shows Parrot using Tortoise's own weapons to end Tortoise's exploitation, at once "sweet-tongued" and coercive, of the birds.

Achebe's *Things Fall Apart* can thus be read as an analysis of the colonial moment in African, Nigerian, and Igbo history in which the traditional folktale of the tortoise and the birds is recoded as an allegory of resistance. In such an allegory, Tortoise represents colonial power. The birds, who are his victims, signify the colonized population that remains subject to manipulation until it learns to command the weapons the colonizers have used against it: words, machetes, spears, and a cannon. The folk wisdom of the animal fable reveals a political message: both rhetoric and armed struggle are crucial to an oppressed people's organized resistance to domination. Ekwefi's tale radically reevaluates folk wisdom, which the tortoise-colonizer uses as a means of subjugation, appropriating custom to legitimize claims to African resources—the "great feast in the sky." Achebe's novel shows that doctrinal, even nostalgic, appeal to "custom" is already anachronistic. Okonkwo's silent and isolated refusal to participate in the collective responses of the village to the European territorial and cultural intrusions represents what Amilcar Cabral has criticized as an unreflective "return to the source" (*Return*). The novel condemns Okonkwo's cultural ahistoricism as self-destructive and self-defeating when Okonkwo commits suicide at the end.

Western critics of the African novel have conventionally focused much of their attention on categories such as traditionalism, folklore, and "primitivism," particularly since the appearance in 1952 of *The Palm-Wine Drinkard* by the Yoruba-Nigerian writer Amos Tutuola. Early reviews in England and the United States consistently placed the work as a "foundling" within the development of world literature. Dylan Thomas, for example, commented in 1952 on the "young English by a West African" and was seconded a year later by Lee Rogow, who described the novel as a "fantastic primitive . . . written in English, but . . . an English with inflections and phrasing which make it seem like a new-born language" (qtd. in Larson, *Emergence* 5, 6). Two decades later, Newton Stallknecht's foreword to Charles Larson's *Emergence of African Fiction* cites these early reviews and reiterates these critical appreciations. Stallknecht heralds Tutuola's novel precisely for what he sees as its lack of historical consciousness, claiming that it "stands out in its exuberant fantasy as *sui generis*, a light that never was on sea or land." For the Western critic, "Tutuola's attitude is undisciplined by a European sense of reality" (x). Stallknecht then contrasts Tutuola's *Palm-Wine Drinkard* with Achebe's first novel, *Things Fall Apart*, which was published six years after Tutuola's work: "Achebe describes, often with shrewd anthropological insight, the moral disintegration of an ancestral order and of an heroic leader brought into collision with European power and ideas" (x–xi).

The dichotomization of a mythical and a historical consciousness, of folklore and historiography, ethnography and art has since embedded itself in academic assessments of non-Western, or nonhegemonic, literatures. Attempts to redress the anthropological bias, such as that of William Lawson, have tended to insist on the "universality" of African literature, assimilating it into a Western valorization of "art for art's sake." Lawson states:

> Early readings of many African novels of the past twenty-five years often seemed to be limited to the sociological information they provided about newsworthy, exotic places. However, it is increasingly apparent that the true significance of many of them lies in the richness of the *universally* meaningful content of the novels, expressing the writers' *intuitive* responses to the world at large as well as to their immediate surroundings.   (20; emphasis added)

This classic dichotomy between ethnographic information and universal insight depoliticizes African literature in the image of the West and thus neutralizes its intervention in the debates, literary-historical as well as socioeconomic, about development and underdevelopment that continue to reinforce the unequal power relations between the "first" and "third" worlds.

We can read *Things Fall Apart* in the context of this debate as a contestatory narrative, an answer to the study presented by the District Commissioner in the last paragraph of the novel. In this study, entitled *The Pacification of the Primitive Tribes of the Lower Niger*, Okonkwo, who has just committed suicide, will be given not a chapter or a novel but a single paragraph (148). By contrast, Okonkwo is the "hero" of Achebe's *Things Fall Apart*. Although his suicide is historical, it is not that of a universal tragic hero, and its necessity derives not from an abstract fate and mythic destiny but rather from a material and ideological crisis in the contemporary history of imperialism. Okonkwo has not learned, as the parrot has, to use language. Nor is he able to participate in the processes of change. He dismisses the parrot's story, which demands the overthrow both of inherited paradigms and of the colonial system, as a tale told by women. Okonkwo's personal failure represents the inadequacy of recalcitrant traditionalism in responding to the exigencies of the present or elaborating a vision of the future.

Achebe, unlike his protagonist Okonkwo, has learned the parrot's lesson. *Things Fall Apart* challenges the authority of Western literary conventions and European colonialism to define an African reality. While acknowledging Europe as part of modern African history—after all, Okonkwo accidentally kills the village boy with an old gun—the novel goes on to indict the presence of the colonizer in West Africa. This indictment elicits a new consideration of the strategies of resistance available to colonial Africa. Like Parrot, and even more effectively than Shakespeare's Caliban, Achebe has learned to use the language.

The language of *Things Fall Apart*, which Bernth Lindfors calls an "African vernacular" and a diction that "simulates the idiom of Ibo, [Achebe's] native tongue," also questions the political and cultural premises of the imperial enterprise ("Palm-Oil" 48). Achebe's use of the folktale, far from being picturesque, operates in a Gramscian sense, as a " 'concept of the world,' to a large extent an implicit one, of a given strata of society . . . in opposition . . . to the 'official' concepts of the world, . . . which have followed each other in the course of historical development" (Gramsci 74). Folklore, then, plays a radically historical role in the unfolding of the novel's plot. As Rems Nna Umeasiegbu points out (6), the plot relies on the folklore motif of punishment[2]—banishment—and enables an inquiry into the politics of nativism on the one hand and aestheticism on the other.

"Among the Ibo," Achebe writes in his novel, "the art of conversation is regarded very highly, and proverbs are the palm-oil with which words are eaten" (5). That very palm oil, the substance of tradition and its transmission, has also become part of West Africa's integration into an international market economy. Palm oil, by the end of the nineteenth century and particularly with the end of the slave trade, had become a major West African export. According to Kannan K. Nair, in his study of southeastern Nigeria between 1841 and 1906, "palm trees which grew wild . . . now had a cash value and oil fetched good prices." Furthermore, "the transition from slave- to oil-exporting produced much social and political change" (30). These same changes are manifest in the Igbo village of Umuofia in Achebe's novel, where the "white man had indeed brought a lunatic religion, but he had also built a trading store and for the first time palm-oil and kernel became things of great price, and much money flowed into Umuofia" (126). As Europe's interest in Africa became more commercialized and as the already distorted and exploitative relations between colonizer and colonized became more bureaucratic, the British had to incorporate Africans into the colonial hierarchy. Frederick Lugard, the British governor general in Nigeria from 1897 to 1919, was responsible for elaborating the system of indirect rule, which used "native agents" to carry out the authority of the British administration. For Lugard,

> in applying the principle of decentralisation, it [was] very essential to maintain a strong central co-ordinating authority, in order to avoid centrifugal tendencies, and the multiplication of units without a sufficiently cohesive bond. . . . (97)

Lugard's "Dual Mandate in British Tropical Africa," written in 1922 after he left Nigeria, and his instructions on colonial administration provide the model for the District Commissioner's dealings with the native population in *Things Fall Apart*. In Achebe's novel, the colonial representation is given another, more critical, paradigm, that of the cunningly eloquent tortoise. The final incidents of Okonkwo's life and the resistant history of the other villagers reenact the fable of the tortoise and the birds. The Commissioner sends "his sweet-tongued messenger to the leaders of Umuofia asking them to meet him in his headquarters" (136). The guileless villagers who gather at the Commissioner's office witness the coercion, humiliation, and brutal violation of six men who "[e]ven when . . . left alone . . . found no words to speak to one another" (138). This incident culminates in Okonkwo's tragic suicide, which causes the people of Umuofia to debate their strategies of resistance to the colonizers' increasing influence. This historically critical incident generates Achebe's novel.

Things Fall Apart, even more than its universal insights or the ethnographic information it provides, contributes to an African literature of resistance. Published in 1958, a year after Ghana became the first African nation to achieve independence, it looks ahead to Nigeria's statehood in 1960 and charts a trajectory of national independence. That independence requires a history of its own, what Eric Hobsbawm calls an "invented tradition," "responses to novel situations which take the form of reference to old situations, or which establish their own past by quasi-obligatory repetition" (2). The tale of the tortoise and the birds is part of such a tradition. In giving and repossessing their feathers, the birds demonstrate their ability to participate in the historical processes of change. Tortoise cannot manage without the help of the birds. The birds' refusal to provide that help, once they understand the conditions it entails, is itself a radical critique of the continued cultural and economic dependency fostered by Europe's "underdevelopment" of Africa (see Rodney).

The tale of the tortoise and the birds is told in many versions in many regions among the many peoples of Africa. It appeals, for example, to the widespread myth of the "flying Africans," whom Vera Kutzinski describes as

> mythical figures which exist outside and in defiance of the authority of the law, which . . . attempts, rather unsuccessfully, to confine them within the limits of a fixed definition or identity, to make them adhere to the conceptual categories officially employed to define reality and truth.   (140)[3]

But the story speaks as well to the many roles assigned to the tortoise by Africa's history of antihegemonic resistance. Writing from a South African prison, Jeremy Cronin finds another injunction in Tortoise's cracked shell. In Cronin's poem "A Tale of Why Tortoise Carries a Hut upon His Back," Tortoise is a prisoner of Tyrannosaurus who brutalizes him and his way of life:

Yet often on return he would find
the small world he'd made was smashed . . .

They say Tortoise is a patient one, yes,
he learnt to be by picking up the fragments of a shattered world
time and time again.

So that's why Tortoise took to carrying
his hut upon his back.
That was long ago.

They tell me Tyrannosaurus is now
extinct,
while Tortoise is alive and well, but you can still see
How he had to stick together broken pieces
—he's got marks on his shell.   (103–04)

Folklorists tend to classify tortoise tales from Africa as "why tales," stories told to explain the past. Achebe's redeployment of the tortoise and the birds and Cronin's version of the tortoise's cracked shell, tales in which the identities of Tortoise, Parrot, and the birds respond to historical exigencies, explain the past as part of an elaboration of possibilities for the future.

NOTES

[1]The status of women in *Things Fall Apart* and Achebe's immanent critique of their traditionally subservient role have not been given significant critical attention. Such an examination would identify women as the main storytellers in the novel, a function that, on the one hand, affirms African women as the bearers and nurturers of African traditions but that, on the other hand, subjects that charge to a new interpretation when these very traditions are rewritten and given a vital assignment within the strategies of African liberation.

[2]This motif is folklore motif Q431 in Stith Thompson's *Motif Index of Folk-Literature*.

[3]I thank Lupenga Mphande and Ana Sisnett, who shared with me their knowledge of the myth and history of tales of "flying Africans."

Things Fall Apart and the Literature of Empire

Hunt Hawkins

By "the literature of empire" I mean works written by European authors that take place in colonies.[1] At Florida State University I have taught honors seminars on this subject for junior English majors and for sophomore liberal studies students. The books I normally use include Joseph Conrad's *Heart of Darkness*, Rudyard Kipling's *Kim*, E. M. Forster's *Passage to India*, George Orwell's *Burmese Days*, Joyce Cary's *Mister Johnson*, and Graham Greene's *Quiet American*. Stretching things a bit, I usually start with Shakespeare's *Tempest*. Although Prospero's island is somewhere in the Mediterranean and is primarily fantastic, the play contains enough references to Bermuda and Indians to make it colonially relevant. Later colonial literature frequently alludes to it, and it inspired O. Mannoni's excellent study of colonial psychology, *Prospero and Caliban*. For similar reasons, I also use Daniel Defoe's *Robinson Crusoe*. Although many readers may remember Crusoe's island as lying in the middle of nowhere, the events of the novel take place within sight of the Venezuelan coast. Crusoe is a staunch colonist who becomes shipwrecked while on a trip to get slaves for his plantation in Brazil. Like Prospero and Caliban, Crusoe and Friday provide a model of the colonial relationship.

Most of the literature of empire, despite these early precursors, belongs to the late nineteenth and early twentieth centuries when colonialism was at its height. Other authors one might use in class are John Buchan, Rider Haggard, Olive Schreiner, C. S. Forester, Somerset Maugham, Isak Dinesen, Elspeth Huxley, Evelyn Waugh, Anthony Burgess, and Doris Lessing. One could also bring in French writers such as Pierre Mille and André Malraux and German writers such as Frieda von Bülow and Hans Grimm.

Since the authors of these novels are Western, the perspective is perforce Western, though both pro- and anti-imperialist points of view are represented. To provide some balance, I include two or three Third World writers, such as R. K. Narayan and Gabriel García Márquez. One novel I always use is Chinua Achebe's *Things Fall Apart*, which the author conceived in part as a reply to the literature of empire. As Achebe told Kofi Awoonor, the novel aims to "set the score right," to counter works like Cary's *Mister Johnson*, and to offer point-by-point refutation of proimperialist arguments (Awoonor 251–52). Interestingly, it also differs from many Western antiimperialist tenets as well. Thus it is an important book to include as a corrective in a course on the literature of empire. By the same token, I think students can better appreciate *Things Fall Apart* by setting it alongside works of colonial fiction.

A chief argument in favor of imperialism is that non-European peoples have no culture or that their culture ranks below European culture on some imagined linear scale. Shakespeare employs the concept of the great chain of being, representing Caliban as an inferior, more emotional creature who must submit to control by the "reasonable" Prospero. Authors have used Charles Darwin's theory of evolution, which Arthur Lovejoy calls a temporalization of the great chain of being, to position non-Europeans at a stage of development Europeans passed through long ago. A common trope from Shakespeare's time onward characterizes non-Europeans as "children." In *Kim*, Kipling intensifies this insult by making his European protagonist a thirteen-year-old child who has to take care of the adult but bumbling lama, the figurative child.

Achebe responds to this proimperialist argument by showing in detail that the Igbo did have a culture—an economy, a religion, systems of government and jurisprudence, kinship relations, marriage ceremonies, proverbs, and folktales. While not technologically advanced, the culture was functioning and viable. It did not need a European "parent." Kipling, in his famous poem "The White Man's Burden," says Europeans must "Fill full the mouth of famine / And bid the sickness cease" (324). But the society in *Things Fall Apart* suffers no famine, and while it cannot cure some diseases (for example, the swelling in Unoka's legs), it manages relatively well (an herbal remedy, for example, helps Ezinma). Kipling also argues that Europeans bring peace to non-Europeans who are squabbling among themselves. But Achebe shows that wars among the Igbo are relatively minor, ritualized affairs, while the Europeans create real violence. In local wars, for instance, Okonkwo brings home only five heads, but the Europeans wipe out the village of Abame. Finally, Kipling calls non-Europeans "Half devil" (321), justifying imperialism in the same way Crusoe justifies the conversion of Friday: that the "heathen" must be Christianized. In Akunna's talks with Mr. Brown, Achebe answers charges that the Igbo worship idols and have no supreme God. Igbo religion is perhaps even superior to Christianity in its integration with everyday life and its lack of puritanical bigotry as personified by Mr. Brown. Unlike Christianity, Igbo religion is not evangelical, and therefore it is not a party to imperialism. (In my experience, evangelical Christian students have the most trouble stomaching Achebe. None ever has, but at least we have had some vigorous discussions.)

Conrad's *Heart of Darkness*, another novel set in Africa of the 1890s, provides an interesting contrast to *Things Fall Apart*. Achebe has publicly attacked Conrad for his demeaning portrayal of Africans (see "Image"; "Viewpoint"). He calls Conrad a "bloody racist" and asserts that *Heart of Darkness* should no longer be taught ("Image" 788). I personally believe Achebe's position is extreme. Close reading of Conrad's novel uncovers a good deal of sympathy for Africans. Although Conrad does use derogatory epithets throughout the book, he still clearly opposes the exploitation of Africans and the interference with their culture. "Savagery," Marlow says, "had a right to exist" (59).

Unlike Achebe, Conrad focuses on the imperialists. While not caricatures,

Achebe's European characters are fairly static. We learn nothing about their personal backgrounds before they come to Africa; we see little change in them once they are there. In contrast, Conrad wants to demonstrate the corruption of the Europeans by imperialism. The company men sink into mindless greed, and the initially idealistic Kurtz plunges beyond greed into other lusts, the most dangerous being his desire to become a god.

Achebe, however, correctly points out that Conrad does very little to portray African culture. None of his African characters has a name. With the exception of Kurtz's mistress, no African appears for more than a paragraph. In fact, Conrad's Africans barely speak, uttering a total of only four sentences. Thus one needs to study the two novels as complementary to each other: Conrad's for its picture of the imperialists, Achebe's for the Africans.

Although Achebe's novel is anti-imperialist, it does not use quite the same arguments as European anti-imperialist works. As I have already suggested, it does not deal with the spiritual harm done to the imperialists, a topic that concerns Conrad, Forster, Orwell, Cary, and Greene. For example, in *Burmese Days*, Orwell's hero Flory commits suicide as a result of his emotional and intellectual isolation after Elizabeth rejects him. One can understand, however, why Achebe is not drawn to this particular anti-imperialist argument: the damage done to Europeans was of a different order than that done to Africans. The psychological destruction of a few individuals has little prominence beside the material exploitation and cultural devastation of entire peoples.

As his title implies, Achebe argues that colonialism causes the African social order to disintegrate. European anti-imperialists have also used this argument, but Achebe differs from them in the balance and objectivity of his presentation. Romantic writers such as Herman Melville in *Typee* tend to see non-Europeans as "noble savages" and their societies as idyllic utopias. In Cary's *Mister Johnson* the title character is a Romantic type (a natural poet), while the society of Fada is viewed as stagnant and corrupt. Cary nonetheless ends up being anti-imperialist because he questions the Western concept of progress: Rudbeck's road only succeeds in enlarging the corruption already present and leads to the tragic demise of Johnson.

In contrast to the novels of empire already discussed by the class, *Things Fall Apart* honestly and dispassionately presents neither a Romantic utopia nor a corrupt backwater. A valuable first step in teaching the novel is to have students discuss the positive and negative aspects of Igbo culture. Some students refuse to see any good, probably because many of the positive aspects reflect Igbo communalism and therefore counter the ingrained individualism of contemporary Americans. Most students will at least recognize the equality of opportunity in the society, and from there they may go on to approve the communal ownership of fallow land that makes this equality possible. Many students also appreciate the strong kinship relations, especially between the generations.

In discussing the negative aspects of the society, my students in recent years, particularly the women, have been upset by its apparent sexism. I counter this objection to a degree by pointing out that while Igbo men practice polygamy and pay a bride price, women are free to divorce and to form relationships based on love (as Ekwefi does, for example). Similarly, while women cannot look at the *egwugwu*, much less be one, they hold some positions of power (as the priestess Chielo does, for example).

Ultimately, however, some aspects of Igbo culture seem patently "bad" —at least to Western eyes. The ostracism of the *osu*, the killing of twins, and the ritual murder of Ikemefuna are difficult to justify to students. Achebe does not directly reveal his feelings about these things because the novel adopts a conventional third-person realism. It reports events without any intrusion of authorial judgment. However, the narrative does behave as if the beliefs of Igbo society are literally true. For example, when Okagbue Uyanwa digs a hole in the compound, he does indeed find Ezinma's *iyi-uwa*. Achebe thus grants the society its assumptions.

The conclusion we are led to is that our value judgments as outsiders are not crucial. The most important truth about Igbo society is that it was once a functioning whole. Components of the society that we may now view as either good or bad were organically interconnected; for example, the same group mentality that fosters strong kinship relations also causes Ikemefuna to be chosen as a victim when the whole village of Mbaino is held responsible for the murder of Udo's wife. The novel thus presents the cultural integrity of the society beyond any value judgments.

Achebe proceeds to show how that integrity was shattered. In their initial incursion the Europeans divided the society by appealing to those members disaffected by its "negative" elements. The missionaries converted the *osu*, the mothers of twins, and Ikemefuna's friend Nwoye, Okonkwo's son. Thus divided, the tribe could not resist. The Europeans took over with relatively little use of force, though they were always backed by its potential. Achebe's vision of Igbo disintegration, the product of Europeans who exploited the "negative" yet functioning elements of a society, provides a uniquely objective and powerful protest against imperialism. His work helps "set the score right" in a course on the literature of empire, books that tend to focus on European imperialists and to romanticize or denigrate non-European people.

NOTE

[1]For the pioneer critical study of the literature of empire, see Susanne Howe's *Novels of Empire*, published in 1949. A number of interesting books have followed,

including Jeffrey Meyers's *Fiction and the Colonial Experience*, Alan Sandison's *Wheel of Empire*, Jonah Raskin's *Mythology of Imperialism*, D. C. R. A. Goonetilleke's *Developing Countries in British Fiction*, M. M. Mahood's *Colonial Encounter*, G. D. Killam's *Africa in English Fiction*, Benita Parry's *Delusions and Discoveries*, Hugh Ridley's *Images of Imperial Rule*, and Martin Green's *Dreams of Adventure, Deeds of Empire*.

The Third World Novel as Counterhistory:
Things Fall Apart and Asturias's *Men of Maize*
Edna Aizenberg

> The Ibo tribe was divided into several clans speaking
> different dialects and lacking any central organization.
> For this reason it has practically no known history
> until after the British occupation.
> > —Alan C. Burns

> When the Spanish undertook the conquest of . . .
> America, [its] peoples were in a state of complete
> decadence. . . . [They] conserve no monument of their
> history . . . nor written laws, only barbaric customs
> and institutions.
> > —Carlos Guzmán-Böckler and Jean Loup Herbert

It is no accident that Chinua Achebe's first novel—a germinative event in modern African writing—is a historical work or that many important novels in Latin America are of the same genre. This homology reflects the shared need of writers to come to terms with a past usurped by a colonial regime —Britain in Nigeria; Spain and its heirs in Spanish-speaking America. To both Africans and Latin Americans, the imaginative re-creation of national history, particularly those portions distorted or censored by the conquerors and their successors, has been directly linked to the concern for national organization. Searching in the past and usually refuting its "official" versions, the novelist meditates on the national present as well as on the shape of things to come.[1] As Achebe writes, "Every literature must seek the things that belong unto its peace . . . [must] evolve out of the necessities of its history, past and current, and the aspirations and destiny of its people" (*Morning* 7).

The historicism of *Things Fall Apart*, then, is far from an isolated phenomenon. It represents a significant mode of narration not only in Africa (witness Ngugi, Armah, and others) but also in other parts of the Third World. Thus a comparative approach to teaching the novel as historical fiction, as counterhistory, is particularly fruitful. By reading *Things Fall Apart* along with a path-breaking Latin American novel similarly concerned with a historical "act of restoration" and the point of view of the vanquished, students gain a greater sense of Achebe's achievement (*Morning* 12). Such a comparison broadens the import of the novel for them, underlining it as a work that shows how fiction—especially the link between fiction and history—is understood in the non-Western world. This comparison further clarifies for students some major questions about the composition of historical fiction in formerly imperialized areas. For example, what historical moments did the authors choose for novelization and why? What is the relation between the novel and the historical moment in which it was written? What (revisionist) view of history does it project? What narrative-linguistic strategies does it employ to elaborate its counterhistory? Furthermore, Achebe's emphasis on the ties between European colonialist ideology and European colonialist rhetoric helps students examine the non-European "rhetoric" writers use to counter the colonizer's ideology (see *Morning* 10).

Men of Maize, written in 1949 by the Guatemalan Nobel Prize winner Miguel Angel Asturias, is a novel that works well in a comparative analysis. I recommend teaching it with *Things Fall Apart* in courses on Third World literature, but the same approach can be used effectively in a variety of other courses: comparative literature (for instance, twentieth-century fiction); masterpieces, in which students gain a great deal by reading masterful non-European writing; history and politics of the developing world (I have successfully incorporated fiction into such offerings); and even African or Latin American literature, courses that can be insular in their own way if they fail to indicate that they share their preoccupations with other cultures "peripheral" to the West. *Men of Maize* compares meaningfully with *Things Fall Apart*, because Asturias's novelistic production has also been cited for its "exemplary value" (Fuentes 24). It is a production—like Achebe's—informed by a concern with the history of the author's people and continent: dictatorship in *El señor presidente* (1946); the penetration of Central America by American economic interests in the "banana trilogy," *Strong Wind* (1950), *The Green Pope* (1954), and *The Eyes of the Interred* (1960); and the invasion of Asturias's homeland by American-backed forces in *Weekend in Guatemala* (1956). *Men of Maize* also deals with the same issue that occupies Achebe in *Things Fall Apart*—the confrontation between the indigenous peoples and the Europeans, a confrontation in which a coherent worldview and way of life are uprooted and replaced with an alien, frequently alienating, socio-cultural-economic system. In this system the "natives," their culture denigrated, must be "pacified," and history must be rewritten to contrast the "inglorious" precolonial past with the "benefits" wrought by Western civilization. Both Asturias and Achebe include scenes of violence in which the Europeans use military force to quell resistance by the Native Americans and the Igbo; both novels also offer explicit accounts of the conquerors' version of history, told by Western characters who are writing about the "primitives."

With this basic parallelism between the two novels in mind, I orient class discussion toward the specific questions I want to address. I work closely with both texts and also assign short oral reports, presented by individual students, on topics connected to the novels.

After student reports on the history of Nigeria and Guatemala and, if possible, the Igbo and Mayan peoples, the class examines the historical moments the authors chose to novelize. Asturias and Achebe selected moments of crisis, junctures at which historical conflicts crystallized. In *Things Fall Apart* Achebe focuses on the initial confrontation between Europeans and Africans. *Men of Maize* suggests that this inaugural clash has been continuously relived in Guatemala, and it departs from one of these repetitions, a late nineteenth-century usurpation of Indian lands that destroyed Indian communities in order to turn Guatemala into an exporter of foodstuffs to the West. In both books, the discord centers on the opposition of individuals and the indigenous civilizations they represent to the subjugators' order: Okonkwo in *Things Fall Apart*; Gaspar Ilóm, the Native American leader, in *Men of Maize.* The authors chose a historical turning point because of its direct implication for the present. Achebe wants "to look back and try and find out where we went wrong, where the rain began to beat us" (*Morning* 44); Asturias seeks to chart the origins and development of the Guatemalan crisis of his day and to propose possible solutions.

Next, the class considers the relation between the novel and its time of composition. Achebe and Asturias wrote at moments of nationalistic awakening, and student reports again provide background information. Students might also read Achebe's description of how the "nationalist movement in British West Africa after the Second World War brought about a mental revolution which began to reconcile us to ourselves" (*Morning* 70). His recreation of a dignified African past in what he characterizes as "the ritual return and homage of a prodigal son" thus directly correlates to the political struggle for independence and a new nationality. (*Things Fall Apart* was published in 1958; Nigeria gained independence in 1960.) Asturias composed *Men of Maize* in a period of nationalist revolutionary fervor in Guatemala (1944–54). When the years of dictatorship ended, Asturias's longtime friend Juan José Arévalo became the democratically elected president. Arévalo and his successor, Jacob Arbenz, undertook to change Guatemala "from a dependent nation with a semicolonial economy to an economically and thus politically independent nation." Aware of "certain prejudices in the social order," of a "lack of sympathy" for the Indians and other groups in a nation three-quarters Indian, the new rulers initiated policies of change, among them the redistribution of land to the dispossessed (E. B. Burns 273, 274). Asturias's novel, which focuses on the Meso-Americans' traditional reverence for the earth and their primary product, maize, offers a literary counterpart to events in the sociopolitical realm. Thus both novels are aesthetic responses to historic change in the direction of national self-assertion.

Class discussion now turns to the revisionist history proposed by the novels. In rejecting the colonialist versions of history, Achebe and Asturias elaborate a counterhistory in which the pre-European past—with all its imperfections—"was not one long nightmare of savagery from which the first Europeans acting on God's behalf delivered [the non-Europeans]"

(*Morning* 45).[2] Neither novelist idealizes the non-European peoples. Achebe clearly identifies the imperfections in Igbo society that facilitated the penetration of the whites, and Asturias often depicts Native Americans with faults of egotism, pettiness, or physical ugliness. Neither writer denies the fact of conquest and domination by the whites, but both works intend to vindicate the wronged. Since every text is a dialogue with previous texts, it is not surprising that both authors "answer" the colonialist history embodied in specific colonialist writings (though it would be inaccurate to see these books as a reply to only one text). In class, one student reports on Joyce Cary's "much praised" novel, *Mister Johnson*, the work Achebe has tried to "deconstruct" (*Morning* 70). I explain that Asturias responds not only to a long series of chroniclers and writers who denigrate the Indians (including himself at an earlier stage) but apparently to a particular article, "Uspantán e Ilóm." The piece tells of a "heroic" attempt by a group of young non-Indians to settle and farm a remote region of Guatemala "much in the way the Europeans had come with the intent of political and military conquest" (the ideological markings could not be less explicit). But the "natives," led by their chief and "medicine man," Gaspar Ilóm, realize that the outsiders would disturb their "sacred backwardness," so they "raise . . . the banner of revolt." The Europeans quell the "revolt" (in which the Indians defend their ancestral lands and way of life) by poisoning the chief and upholding the "rights" granted to them by the government ("Uspantán," my translation). In the novel, Asturias retells the revolt from the point of view of the Indians: Ilóm's death begins a process that brings pain and suffering to his people but at the same time permits them to take revenge on the usurpers and to ultimately (and utopically) return to their land.

To introduce the class to the linguistic-narrative strategies used in historical revisionism, I read from "The African Writer and the English Language," in which Achebe quotes a paragraph from *Arrow of God* as it would sound first in African English, then in standard English. I then read examples of "African" English from Cary's novel. In attempting to rewrite the caricature of the Africans and their history presented by writers like Cary, Achebe emphasizes the importance of language: "No man can understand another whose language he does not speak (and 'language' here does not mean simply words, but a man's entire world view)" (*Morning* 48). A dignified presentation of Africans cannot be made in the laughable English they frequently speak in European novels: "Oh, Mister Rudbeck is jess the fines' man in de worl' " (Cary 25). Achebe counters the colonialists' linguistic denigration of the African by consciously building an English that conveys the African experience and stresses the importance of words in African and other so-called primitive societies (see "Language and the Destiny of Man" and "The African Writer and the English Language"). This strategy involves techniques such as use of African syntactical structures, turns of phrase, and metaphors; use of proverbs, verbal constructs typical to Igbo society; emphasis on the Igbo regard for the art of conversation and on conversation in the novel; and use of the linguistic-narrative resources of the African song, folktale, and myth traditions. Indeed, the myths and sacred tales of the Igbo are, as Achebe underscores, an "attempt to make sense of the bewildering complexity of existence" (*Morning* 35); thus these traditions—as words and as a worldview—are essential for the verisimilar re-creation of precolonial African society. (Achebe's interest in African myth is evident in many of his essays, including "Chi in Igbo Cosmology.")

Men of Maize creates a new language to reinvent the past. Like Achebe, Asturias calls on the rhetorical resources of traditional society to effect this invention. Achebe, while making full use of these resources, is still well within a realistic framework, and he tries to document the details of Igbo life and Igbo cosmology without exaggeration or distortion (in part as an answer to colonialist writers' wild flights of fancy about African primitivism and black magic [JanMohamed, *Manichean Aesthetics*]). Asturias, however, delves deep into the myth world of the Meso-Americans, using its magic language to write and structure his novel. Beginning with the title metaphor, which is based on the Mayan myth that recounts how the gods created humanity out of maize, the work's organization, symbols, and images are inspired by such sacred pre-Columbian texts as the *Popol Vuh* and the *Book of Chilam Balam*. (Both texts are suitable topics for student reports.) Asturias greatly modifies the linear, "logical" presentation of the realist Western novel, immersing the reader in the worldview of the Indians, a "telluric" world close to nature (Guibert 137–39). In this way, he succeeds in "personalizing" the "anonymous people of Guatemala" (Fuentes 24). Asturias's work relies more heavily on the mythic and oneiric than Achebe's does because of the influence of surrealism on Asturias; the challenge of the social sciences, which had begun to document Native American reality more fully and to make novelistic documentation less necessary; and the failure of earlier Indianist novels to penetrate Native American psychology through external description of Indian "folkways."

A comparative examination of *Things Fall Apart* and *Men of Maize* enriches and expands the study of Achebe's novel, setting it within the context of the concerns and strategies of modern Third World literature. Students learn from this approach that Achebe, while speaking for himself, his people, and Africa, also speaks for much of the world outside Europe and North America. They get a sense that other major writers in the Third World share Achebe's literary concerns; indeed, Achebe's skillful expression of essential issues— particularly the issue of reclaiming one's history—makes his novel a major work. Despite the differences between *Things Fall Apart* and *Men of Maize*, students come out of the course with a keener awareness of the commonality of spirit among Third World writers, who increasingly participate in a dialogue with one another, as well as with their own traditions and the West. As Africans search for cultural independence from Europe, they have looked more than once to a fruitful exchange of ideas with Latin America: Achebe himself cites the Chilean poet Pablo Neruda as a role model for African writers (*Morning* 27). An African–Latin American approach to teaching *Things Fall Apart* is itself a contribution to that dialogue.

NOTES

[1]The ongoing importance in Latin America of refuting "official" versions of history through artistic means can be seen from the successful Argentine film *La historia oficial* ("The Official Story/History"—the double meaning of the Spanish word is fully played on in the title). The movie aims to penetrate the authorized version of Argentina's not-too-distant history, when thousands of people disappeared under military rule.

[2]See Knipp for a useful discussion of fictional counterhistories in recent African writing.

CHALLENGING APPROACHES

Making Men and History:
Achebe and the Politics of Revisionism

Rhonda Cobham

While Western student readers of *Things Fall Apart* complain that the novel is "sexist"—meaning usually that they find Okonkwo misogynistic—African student readers are more likely to praise Achebe and chastise other Igbo writers like Buchi Emecheta for not being as authentic as Achebe in portraying traditional Igbo women. Both comments imply that some truly objective, unbiased version of traditional life exists and that the writer's duty is to deliver it to readers in a way that engages our sympathies for the "right" causes and stimulates our imaginations in the "right" directions.

Achebe probably had an agenda in writing his novel quite different from that of either the Western or the African readers who now study it. The son of a village catechist and the winner of scholarships to secondary school and then to the newly established University College, Ibadan, Achebe belongs to the first generation of African writers to be familiar from early childhood with Western and indigenous traditions. The eloquent oral traditions of the Igbo community as well as the compelling prose of the King James Bible imbued him with a love of language and an appreciation of the timing and cadence of a well-wrought sentence. The texts that formed his vision of Africa, however, were novels like Joyce Cary's *Mister Johnson* and Joseph Conrad's *Heart of Darkness*, texts Achebe says he read with resistance (see "Image"). Like his modern African readers, he could see the ways in which his Christian family's values differed from or coincided with those of more traditional Igbo families. Like his Western readers, he must have been uncomfortably aware that many of the traditions still influencing his life would have been considered brutal or misogynistic from the perspective of the fictive author of *The Pacification of the Primitive Tribes of the Lower Niger*.

Unlike both groups of readers and, indeed, unlike either of the cultures to which they had access, Achebe's generation of African intellectuals had no readily available symbolic discourse through which they could simultaneously represent and ascribe value to the various cultural influences that had formed them. To be sure, they could quote Yeats and Eliot to one another in one breath and spar with traditional proverbs in the next, but who besides them would get the joke? Who in the community that had come before them or that was likely to come after them would understand and give full value to all aspects of their accomplishments and ways of seeing? In *Things Fall Apart*, Okonkwo voices a similar angst when, in a rare moment of solidarity with his father, he contemplates the defection of his eldest son, Nwoye, to the Christians:

> Suppose when he died all his male children decided to follow Nwoye's steps and abandon their ancestors? Okonkwo felt a cold shudder run through him at the terrible prospects, like the prospect of annihilation. He saw himself and his fathers crowding round their ancestral shrine waiting in vain for worship and sacrifice and finding nothing but ashes of bygone days, and his children the while praying to the white man's god. (108)

In the rhetoric of our age we would say that both Okonkwo and his creator are concerned with the construction of a personal, in this case masculine, identity through which to mediate their connections to past, present, and future communities. Okonkwo's quest is easily charted. Because his father's anomalous life-style deprives him of an inheritance of land, yam seed, or junior wives, he has access to no material objects that can provide him with a reference for who he is or what he may become. His most immediate point of male reference, his father, is described by the society as *agbala*, a word that "could . . . mean a man who had taken no title" but that also meant "woman" (10). Like Mary Shelley's monster in *Frankenstein*, Okonkwo must fabricate a social context for his identity and values rather than simply assume a system of references in relation to which he can define himself. He creates this context by isolating and responding to specific symbols of masculinity within his culture as if they, in the abstract, could constitute all that he needs to construct his social self.

The pivotal example of this process in the novel is Okonkwo's understanding of the concept of courage. At the outset it is the masculine attribute most immediately accessible to him, as it seems wholly contingent on his performance as an individual. The opening paragraphs of the novel define Okonkwo in terms of his courage when he throws Amalinze the Cat in wrestling. Later we discover that Okonkwo's courage on this occasion immediately translates into an affirmation of his social identity since it wins him the love of a woman he is not yet "man enough," in terms of material wealth, to marry.

Such early instances of social recognition for his courage are compounded over the years as Okonkwo struggles "manfully" against bad weather and poor harvests to acquire his own yam seed and as he takes lives in battle. Gradually, for Okonkwo, prestige and manliness become synonymous with the ability to do difficult, even distasteful, jobs without flinching. When the Oracle demands the life of his ward, Ikemefuna, Okonkwo finds himself without access to a system of values that would allow him to distance himself from the killing of the child who "calls [him] father" and remain a man (40). He strikes the blow that kills the child, offending the earth goddess, Ala, and setting in motion a chain of events that ultimately leads to his downfall.

Okonkwo's limited understanding of physical ascendancy as courage and his equation of courage with masculinity are set against the richer and more complex values available to his clan as a whole. In the novel, Okonkwo's friend Obierika advocates this greater tradition. The narrative structurally reinforces Obierika's words by juxtaposing Okonkwo's actions and those of other members of the society in a way that invites us to consider the complexity of the clan's values. Thus, Okonkwo sees tenderness as incompatible with masculinity, viewing marriage as yet another social situation in which a man measures his worth by his ability to control others through superior physical strength. But Achebe makes readers aware of the ways the community qualifies such notions of male prerogative. Okonkwo's response to the almost simultaneous deaths of Ndulue and his wife Ozoemena dramatizes the gap between his personal code and that of the clan as a whole:

> "It was always said that Ndulue and Ozoemena had one mind," said Obierika. "I remember when I was a young boy there was a song about them. He could not do anything without telling her."
> "I did not know that," said Okonkwo. "I thought he was a strong man in his youth."
> "He was indeed," said Ofoedu.
> Okonkwo shook his head doubtfully.
> "He led Umuofia to war in those days," said Obierika.   (47–48)

Okonkwo himself is punished when he breaks the Week of Peace and beats his wife, a judgment that reflects a symbolic recognition of wife beating as violence even though it may also be associated with legitimate masculine privilege. The ruling of the *egwugwu*, who unequivocally censure the chronic batterer Uzowulu, shows that the community draws a line between physical prowess and bullying, courage and cowardice.

Okonkwo's most complex conflation of brute force with the "masculine" virtue of courage occurs in the final pages of the story, when he beheads the court messenger and then hangs himself. Here courage is dissociated from those other "manly" attributes: caution, diplomacy, and the ability to weigh both sides of an argument. Ironically, none of these "higher" values in his society has any effect on the superior military might of the colonizers. Thus, in a twisted sense, Okonkwo and the District Commissioner share the same worldview: that, ultimately, physical strength and the ability to inflict one's will on another human being—a wife, a son, or a native—are the only significant forms of social differentiation in establishing a masculine identity.

The act of suicide symbolically marks the parting of the ways between Okonkwo and his clan. Until that act, he accepts the censure of his community for his unpremeditated acts of violence, because at heart he accepts that their universe encompasses his. Faced with the whispered comment "Why did he do it?" after he kills the messenger, Okonkwo finally decides that his clan no longer share his values and that to be a man on their terms would be a form of living death (145). His community reciprocates his final act of distancing, denying him a proper burial. And yet Okonkwo characteristically underestimates the flexibility and comprehensiveness of the clan's values. When Obierika declares, "That man was one of the greatest men in Umuofia," he extends to Okonkwo the same complex and qualified acceptance accorded to Ndulue, who was great but unable to do anything without telling his wife (147). Thus the accolade of manhood is conferred on Okonkwo even in default, both in the words of his friend and in the act of narration that constitutes Achebe's novel.

Okonkwo's final solution brings us back to the dilemma of his creator. Like Okonkwo, who attempts to carve out a relation to his clan in the absence of an inherited sense of identity, Achebe must renegotiate a relation to traditional Igbo society, a connection his education, religious training, and internalized moral standards have made tenuous. Like Okonkwo, he often proceeds by isolating specific aspects of a society to which he has access and allowing them to stand for many other possible readings of a given social situation. Achebe has said that his mission in writing *Things Fall Apart* is to teach other Africans that their past was neither so savage nor so benighted as the colonizers have represented it to be. In other words, Achebe wants to prove to himself that the best values of his Christian upbringing are compatible with the values of traditional Igbo society.

Things Fall Apart selectively incorporates many supposedly Western or Christian values into the celebration of the traditional way of life. I would like to discuss briefly three examples: the killing of Ikemefuna, the representation of marriage, and the selective elaboration of women's roles within traditional Igbo society.

In describing Ikemefuna's death, Achebe, like Okonkwo, must find a way of synchronizing the qualities he wishes to represent with the values he has internalized. While Achebe shares the mission-school horror at the idea of human sacrifice, an attitude he also attributes to the converts in *Things Fall Apart*, he must find ways of addressing this issue without jeopardizing the reader's sympathy for the community as a whole. Thus he structures the story of Ikemefuna's death so that it parallels the biblical story of Abraham's near sacrifice of his son Isaac. The journey out of the village, the boy's carrying of the vessels associated with the sacrifice, and his last disarming words, "My father, they have killed me!" all echo the biblical story (43). Isaac performs each act attributed to Ikemefuna, uttering his own last disarming remark: "My father . . . behold the fire and the wood: but where is the lamb . . ." (Gen. 22.7). The major difference, of course, is that no ram substitutes for Ikemefuna. Yet we feel sure that, just as Abraham would have killed his son had the ram not been caught in the thicket, Okonkwo would have spared his, had a ram materialized for him. Both fathers act in strict obedience to their gods, and both contemplate the deed they must perform with horror as well as fortitude.

Okonkwo's situation also parallels the New Testament story about God's sacrifice of his son Jesus for the greater good of all humanity (itself a version of the Abraham-Isaac motif). Achebe picks the form of human sacrifice most compatible with Judeo-Christian myth as the centerpiece of his examination of human sacrifice in Igbo culture. The more ubiquitous forms, such as "throwing away" twins in the bad bush or killing slaves when their owners die, are mentioned only in passing, as evils already under fire within traditional society and whose eradication is hastened by the coming of the missionaries. For Achebe's readers to share the tragedy of Ikemefuna's death as a moment of pathos rather than one of revulsion, the parallel with Abraham must function as a shared archetype. The object of sacrifice must be a sentient individual, bound to the person who makes the sacrifice by bonds of affection. In this way the act of sacrifice becomes a symbol of devotion to a principle higher than earthly love rather than the brute machination of a culture incapable of elevated sentiments. Though Okonkwo's personal intervention in Ikemefuna's death remains tragically wrongheaded, the context in which he acts retains its dignity.

Achebe reinforces such parallels in his story with thematic strategies in the conversations between the enlightened missionary Mr. Brown and the enlightened Igbo villager Akunna. We may read their conversations as a metaphor for Achebe's search for a point of convergence between the two codes that inform his ethics. Similarly, his description of what attracts Nwoye to the Christians reflects his strategy with the reader, that of using biblical myth to reinforce Igbo values. As he points out, "It was not the mad logic of the Trinity that captivated [Nwoye]. He did not understand it. It was the poetry of the new religion, something felt in the marrow" (104).

On the personal and political levels, Achebe's representation of women within Igbo society follows a similar pattern. Although the novel tells us of Okonkwo's many wives and children, the male-female relationships in Okonkwo's family that Achebe isolates for our scrutiny are almost indistinguishable from those of monogamous couples in Western tradition. Okonkwo has three wives, but we come to know only one: Ekwefi, the mother of Ezinma. She marries Okonkwo for love, having run away from her first husband. Her relationship with her husband, for better or worse, has all the passion, violence, and shared trauma we associate with the Western romantic tradition. Achebe clearly intends to show that all these emotions existed in traditional Igbo society, but, as with the situation he chooses to illuminate the issue of human sacrifice, the relationship he describes between Okonkwo and Ekwefi is by no means normative. We never really see Okonkwo's wives interacting with one another the way we see the men interacting among themselves or even Okonkwo interacting with his children. From a Western perspective the omission is hardly experienced as a loss, as the reader can identify effortlessly with the structure if not the content of the relationship described between Okonkwo and Ekwefi. Indeed, its similarity to Western versions of marriage may help explain why students spontaneously empathize with Ekwefi when Okonkwo mistreats her and why they often read the text as misogynistic. By contrast, they seem to have much more difficulty understanding the friendly alliances between senior and junior wives in the work of Flora Nwapa. Many students reject outright the idea in Ama Ata Aidoo's Anowa that a wife could actively seek a junior wife for her husband as a way of marking her material consequence or asserting her identity. Such relationships are important in constructing female identity, and that is clearly not what Achebe's novel is about.

A similar selective process occurs in the representation of women's public roles. Achebe names one of the two groupings within the clan that endowed women with specific political authority: the *umuada*, or daughters of the clan (93). Since Igbo marriage ties were usually exogamous, a woman also belonged to another group in her husband's village consisting of the wives of the clan. Directly or indirectly, these groups controlled between them many aspects of civic and familial life. In *Things Fall Apart*, these groups police stray animals (80), solemnize certain stages of marriage and betrothal rituals (92–93), and preserve maternal lines of land entitlement (91, 94–95). Indeed, Okonkwo's survival in exile hinges on his right to exercise his entitlement to land in his mother's village via the connections vested in her as a wife in Okonkwo's clan and as a daughter in her father's clan.

Achebe does not tell us, however, that the *umuada* also regulated the markets in each town and that they intervened or threatened to intervene to settle civic as well as marital disputes. When Uzowulu is brought to judgment for chronic abuse of his wife, one of the elders asks why such a minor matter has been brought to the attention of the *egwugwu*. Another elder replies, "Don't you know what kind of man Uzowulu is? He will not listen to any other decision" (66). Achebe clearly introduces the *egwugwu* here to underline for his audience in terms they can appreciate how seriously the community looks on violence against women. But anthropological accounts indicate that, in a more likely scenario, the wives of the clan would have intervened and enforced their judgment by "sitting" on the man in question: that is, by shaming him publicly through rude songs and obscene gestures so that he would be forced to mend his ways. Alternatively, the female kinswomen of the battered woman who had married into the clan of the offending male could have threatened to enforce a sexual strike if their husbands did not see to it that Uzowulu corrected his behavior.[1]

Achebe would, no doubt, have been hard put to imbue such scenarios with the decorum expected of women in Western tradition. Indeed, he may have internalized a Western view of legal authority, defining male courts of law as the ultimate seats of power in any society, to such an extent that alternative ways of dramatizing Uzowulu's ostracism through female intervention may have seemed ineffective by comparison. In any event, these omissions leave us with no example of female authority in the Igbo social structure that is not compatible with traditional Western ideals of women as nurturing, ornamental, or needing protection. A truly jaundiced eye would also have to note that the novel describes women cooking, plaiting their hair, decorating their bodies, dancing, running from *egwugwu*, and being given in marriage. We do not see them planting their farms, bartering their goods in the marketplace, sitting in judgment on members of their community, or taking action alongside or against their men. The only woman we see acting with any authority is the priestess of Chielo, and she is represented, in terms consistent with Western practice, as a witch—a force for good or evil who is separate from the regular women rather than part of a chain of ritual and social female authority.

Such omissions become all the more difficult to reconcile when one considers the Women's War in Aba in 1929. This revolt, organized by the wives and daughters of a number of Igbo clans, had delivered one of the most sweeping challenges to colonial authority in living memory at the time when Achebe was writing. In fact, this event motivated the British government to give research grants to several "amateur" colonial anthropologists to study Igbo society specifically. These studies produced the spate of early anthropological accounts that Achebe satirizes in his reference to the District Commissioner's projected book *The Pacification of the Primitive Tribes of the Lower Niger*.[2]

If Achebe had avoided this selective process and paid closer attention to women's political structures within Igbo society, one scene in the novel would, in my opinion, have been richer. When Okonkwo flees to his mother's homeland after committing the female crime of manslaughter, his maternal uncle lectures him on the importance of the feminine principle in Igbo culture. Okonkwo, who can only define masculinity in relation to what his father was *not*, understandably balks at the notion that his identity may also be formed by qualities represented by his mother. But because we as readers have no sense of the full range of qualities—both protective and assertive —that are associated with the feminine principle in Igbo society, we are as limited in interpreting the scene as Okonkwo is. We know that he should be patient and dependent and grateful for the protection of his mother's homeland. We also know that in spiritual terms the earth goddess Ala is the deity Okonkwo has most often offended and that she is responsible for his exile. However, we have no way of knowing that the female power Ala symbolizes is represented in the clan by a system of legal codes and practices controlled by women; we also cannot see that by refusing the comfort of his mother's homeland Okonkwo also rejects the very civic culture that regulates, in part, his access to the privileges of manhood. Achebe implies many of these ideas in this scene, but the scene lacks the rich nuances that characterize the unfolding of masculine systems of values and authority.

Achebe's selective use of those aspects of Igbo traditional society that best coincide with Western-Christian social values speaks to his own need to establish a worldview, both modern and traditional, of which he can be a part. To call the way he treats the formation of masculine identity sexist is a facile and not very accurate reading of a gendered response to a specific cultural dilemma. That Achebe's narrative is indeed a selective, gendered one that partakes of both traditional and Judeo-Christian patriarchal values becomes a problem only in the light of the novel's historical reception as the definitive, "objective" account of the Igbo, not to say African, traditional past. In expanding a hypothetical paragraph in a district commissioner's text into the saga of a lost civilization, Achebe imaginatively addresses the nostalgia, social insecurity, and nationalist sentiments of an entire continent. But because of its great success, his representation of the past has become a substitute for a reality that, inevitably, is far more complex than one novel could hope to make it. Like the institutions it helped debunk, Achebe's text has itself become the object of deconstructive exercises in the work of more recent Nigerian writers. In the work of Buchi Emecheta, Achebe's chapters (or perhaps extended paragraphs?) on the position of women in Igbo society have been revised to offer a more complete alternative vision of the attitudes of traditional women to their status in the society. Emecheta offers a partisan and revisionist picture, one committed to challenging Igbo and Judeo-Christian values from the perspective of an upwardly mobile traveler in the women's movement. This perspective, however, must also resist the temptation to limit the roles it ascribes to women in traditional society to those "invented" by Achebe. Indeed, for the modern woman writer in Africa, Achebe's authority must seem as compelling and as difficult to challenge as the district commissioner's voice must have seemed to Achebe in his time.

This irony serves to remind us that literature, like anthropology or history, is a form of selective representation, replete with its inherent assumptions about authenticity and "objectivity." Whether we teach *Things Fall Apart* as an appendix to anthropological and sociological documents or as a way of bringing history to life, we must remember that this particular fiction is a response to history that mimics the structure and claims to objectivity of "science" without for a moment abdicating its right as fiction to be selective, subjective, or unrealistic. Those of us who teach *Things Fall Apart* as literature in the hope of reaffirming traditional values may do well to bear in mind that the values we discover in the text are most likely our own. Achebe's novel is a brilliant resolution of the conflict experienced by his generation between traditional and Western notions of manhood, courage, and the construction of communal values. Such resolution is seldom if ever about choosing between two clearly defined alternatives, and it inevitably involves a process of selection. When our students accuse Achebe of sexism or Emecheta of historical inaccuracy, their statements attest to the creation, for better or worse, of an African literary canon. This canon is based on a highly selective system of values, shared by Achebe and his cohort of African intellectuals, that has come to be used as a way of reading history: a touchstone for the literature as well as for the society of the postcolonial age. Time, perhaps, to change *Things Fall Apart*'s name to *Things Are Consolidated*?

NOTES

[1]Mazi E. N. Njaka lists *umuada* as one of the names for daughters "in their capacity as a women's council. Their duty is to guard against anything that may disturb the orderly nature of Igbo cultural life, particularly when things are not normal and there are violations of the constitution" (158). Njaka lists the Women's Rebellion of 1929 and the Women's Riots of 1957 as two well-known instances of violent political action taken by *umuada* in a range of Eastern communities but also cites the intervention of one *umuada* as late as 1961 to discipline corrupt politicians in the 1961 elections. Njaka sees the *umuada* as "potentially the most powerful organ in the state. Despite this power, however, the Umuada are said to be like mothers—always lenient and not so fierce as they sound" (124). This dual aspect of their political character—as

both tender and terrifying—seems obscured by Achebe's selective portrayal of women's roles.

[2]Sylvia Leith-Ross's *African Women* is the best known of these anthropological studies. It contains an extensive preface explaining how both government and private research foundations came to take a specific interest in Igbo women after the Aba Riots of 1929. Other studies of the region undertaken in the wake of the riots include those by Perham, Meek, and Green (*Land Tenure*).

The Postcolonial African Novel and the Dialogic Imagination

Zohreh T. Sullivan

The problem with teaching *Things Fall Apart* is that though it looks like a traditional realistic novel, it is not. Students respond both with complaints (the novel was too simple, the narrative voice and story too direct, the characters too flat, the resolution and closure too speedily achieved) and with puzzlement that Achebe wrote in the language of the colonizer for the colonizer. My job as teacher is to speak to both reactions: to question the notion that the work is a traditional Western novel and to contextualize it so that its parts make sense. My students sometimes want a visceral engagement with a fully developed realistic hero to help them "understand" the crisis of soul Achebe eloquently describes in his essays and interviews. I begin teaching the novel, therefore, by telling the students who come to class with a simple disappointment that they should be prepared to leave the novel with a complex disappointment. My role as teacher is to complicate the lives of students and their act of reading, not to leave them with resolutions, closures, or the illusion of total knowledge. This essay links methodology and ideology and suggests that criticism and theory finally return us to our beginnings—to accepting the novel at the level of student rejection.

Some student responses to the novel suggest problems of reading, of wanting to know something about Igbo tribal culture at the turn of the century. I draw a chart on the board (adapted from Wren, *Achebe's World*) describing some aspects of Igbo culture and life and ask students if it satisfies their desire for information. It does not. This absence of satisfaction raises problems for the reader, who, composed of "a plurality of other texts," then encounters a text whose plurality defies expectations (Barthes 148). The absence of satisfaction also creates questions about literature, which structuralism contends is not a direct communication from one well-meaning heart or one well-wrought urn to another but a form or code produced by the cultural institution of literature. Achebe's text only frustrates if we search it for the key that will allow us to colonize the novel into our proprietary knowledge, but a look at its structure and some of its cultural codes may help us see it as a product of colonization riddled with the contradictions and polarized values of its cultures.

Mikhail Bakhtin defines the novel as the orchestration of diverse and dialogically opposed social voices of an era. I use this definition in my courses on the novel, whether they focus on British, colonial, or Third World texts,[1] to lay the groundwork for our eventual need to historicize those voices and the dialectic between them. In our study of *Things Fall Apart*, we interrogate the "unity" of style, voice, point of view, and character and work toward an understanding of the split between voices produced by the African epic tradition and by colonial teaching. We also investigate the differences between the oral epic mode (proverbs, paratactic style, masculine narrative, monologic voice, insistence on character as type) and its disturbance by the mode of the historical novel (see JanMohamed, "Sophisticated").

This second mode deserves special attention, particularly in a class on colonialism and the novel, as an example of the decolonization and recolonization of the English language. Achebe is himself a construct of colonial power, a missionary education, a Christian family, and a grandfather who welcomed the earliest missionaries to Ogidi. In writing the tribe's story, he denies the traditional mode of tribal communication and chooses instead an alien Western form, the novel, whose discourse is necessarily linked to Western power, Western forms, and Western images. The novel's intertextuality begins with the title's self-conscious allusion to Yeats's "Second Coming"; it weaves its way into the narrator's use of the epic and lyric style and turns up in unexpected allusions that mark the narrator as one so educated by colonial power that an allusion to Tennyson's "In Memoriam"—"nature . . . red in tooth and claw" (9)—slips in as naturally and unobtrusively as Igbo proverbs and stories.

The internalization of an imposed and alien language has been discussed by contemporary writers such as Ngugi wa Thiong'o and Achebe. My purpose here is not to continue that debate (although we do in class) but to reread the problem in terms of the discourse necessary to the novel as genre and in terms of Bakhtin's notion that language is neither neutral nor private property but always "populated—overpopulated—with the intentions of others" (294). The unitary, monologic voice is an illusion of a primitive or authoritarian culture blinded to the inherently dialogic nature of all utterance: all words are born in response to other words and other languages. Bakhtin writes:

> The internal politics of style (how the elements are put together) is determined by its external politics (its relationship to alien discourse). Discourse lives, as it were, on the boundary between its own context and another, alien, context.   (284)

African writers who use English are aware that their language is already populated with the political, social, and literary intentions of their colonial teachers, but they compel it "to serve [their] own new intentions, to serve a second master" (300).

My approach to teaching the novel is to encourage the class to locate patterns of structure informing the narrative, the characters, and the action; to question these patterns; and to draw connections among structure, style, and ideology. Finally, we focus on the denial and suppression of the feminine and outcast. This fault, shared by both the hero and his culture, dismantles their coherence, thereby allowing the colonizer to possess the hero's son and the land.

After an introductory lecture in which I display maps of Africa and Nigeria and provide background information on stages of colonization and decolonization, we start with the students' general reactions to the plot and story: I ask the class if the plot reminds them of anything else they have read. The inevitable mention of the Greek epic creates an opportunity to discuss the African oral epic tradition and such tales as the medieval epic of Mali, *Sundiata*, whose emphasis on heroism, exile, destiny, and encounters between cultures connects it thematically with Achebe's novel and with the Greek epic. This topic, however, inadvertently leads us to acknowledge the complexity of sources, all of which share a common structural design—of equilibrium or contract destroyed by transgression or violation followed by punishment. Pursuing this structural reading a bit further, we focus on the binary oppositions in Igbo culture and read their versions of universal and timeless polarities between masculine and feminine, earth and sky, the strong and the weak, and the chiefs and the outcasts. Discussion questions handed out before class ask students to chart oppositions in the design, imagery, and structure of the novel, a task that (as in the work of Lévi-Strauss) clarifies the culture's boundaries and values as determined by the language of the text. My students, however, quickly find themselves chafing against the limits of polarity and structuralism, and they begin to thematize and historicize tensions and conflicts on levels of genre, structure, and language.

We engage in a close reading of chapter 1, which introduces problems of kinship, culture, psychology, and ideology. A chapter that begins with Okonkwo and ends with Ikemefuna suggests an Oedipal, mythic narrative concerned with ritual sacrifice: the male hero (and tribe) who violates female laws (*agbala*) is punished. With much help from Robert Wren (*Achebe's World*), we focus on the polarized values that structure event, imagery, and character. We find ourselves becoming deconstructionists, however, as we recognize instabilities and disturbances in the surface structures, unity of purpose, and authorial intent, as well as uncertainties in the notions of origin and coherence. The object of deconstructing a text, as Catherine Belsey reminds us, is to "examine the process of its production," to recognize it as a construct, "and so to treat it as available for deconstruction" (104). In examining the uncertainties in a text, we include the historically specific formations responsible for its shape, and this process too becomes part of the meeting ground for deconstruction and history.

For example, the first event in the opening paragraph, the wrestling match, prepares us for a culture that valorizes the masculine spirit of competition and physical prowess and for an author who chooses to represent that culture through this particular ideologically charged representation. The narrative stance, that of the African epic bard, is distant and single-minded in its understanding of communal values, of time, of individual heroism. But the narrator's voice does not maintain the remoteness of this stance. The chapter moves from the flat, single-voiced recollection familiar to the world of legend to the disturbed, multivoiced description familiar to the world of history. The timeless ceremonies of the kola and the chalk, the wrestling match, and Igbo proverbs encounter the disturbance of individual choice that determines history: Unoka chooses to be *agbala* and to follow his desires that are feminine. History redeems and resurrects this choice in Unoka's grandson Nwoye and in the Christianity that wins the hearts of outcasts and mothers of twins.

The enumeration of Okonkwo's successes frames the repressed story of his failed father, Unoka. The oppositions between the son and the father introduce a narrative and a culture defined by duality. Although the son attempts to resolve that duality, he finds the same pattern threatening him at each stage of his life. Okonkwo's fame, anger, aggression, and violence are opposed by his father's failure, gentleness, laziness, and love of music. We can interpret the scene in which Okoye visits Unoka (as Wren has in *Achebe's World*) in terms of the culture's ability to curb conflict through ceremony. But the underside to this charming rendition of social order is the sinister insistence on maintaining order that results in Ikemefuna's sacrificial death.

So far, however, our analysis of the novel has involved what Bakhtin, Ian Watt, and Northrop Frye would refer to as a centripetal, inward-turning method of interpretation relatively free from engagement with time. Our next and more important tasks are to read the novel historically, to make ourselves aware of the dialogue between the novel and its historic context, and to see the novel as part of an intended trilogy about Igbo history. I inform the class of the historic incident that occurred on 16 November 1905—the killing of J. F. Stewart that provoked the destruction of villagers a month later, which in turn led to "pacification" in the form of the Bende-Onitsha hinterland expedition that prepared the way for colonial takeover. By introducing historical facts, I do not mean to suggest that we should read literature in terms of history as a fixed backdrop of meaning; that would reduce literature to a stepchild of history. Rather I aim to show that Achebe's text is produced and created by a historically specific series of cultural and social formations and that the formal design of the novel, its events, language, character, and narrative are all part of the protean shape of history as Achebe constructs it. Achebe, after all, has shaped our perception of Nigeria and therefore has helped create history. Our task, then, is to examine his particular construction of history as it relates to the discourse of the novel, to see how some parts of his narrative oppose dominant imperial ideology while other parts recuperate its assumptions.

We discuss scenes that work as variations on the motifs of the opening chapter to understand their conscious and unconscious ideological work. Our aims here are to see how African and colonial culture chose to deal with disobedience to the rules of authority; to see how Achebe, a construct of both cultures, mediates between the laws of his dual ancestry, in the process turning a horrendous transgression into a palatable story; and to see the significance of the unconscious contradiction between gendered values in African and Christian contexts as an opening into historical contradictions and the problem of ideological representation. The coming of Ikemefuna, the beating of Ojiugo, the killing of Ikemefuna, *agbala*, the story of Ozoemena, and the functions of Obierika, Nwoye, and art—all these events and ideas occur on a manifest level of privileged masculine activity that recalls the monologic epic thrust of the original narrative voice. Yet these scenes include unofficial, "female"-*agbala* voices that oppose and disrupt the surface action, thereby creating the confrontational heteroglossia of the novel. Although the novel's form and its arrangements of characters center on Okonkwo, the elements Okonkwo represses—the feminine, the weak, and the gentle—erupt to assault and defy his authority (the death of Ikemefuna), his family (the defection of Nwoye), and the clan (the coming of the missionaries). The elements denied in the self (the feminine and outcast) are also denied by the clan, who condemn twins and outcasts into the Evil Forest to die. But the denied and repressed gain narrative force as they destroy the repressor, who, in the first half of the epic and oral narrative, is Okonkwo. Ironically, in the second half of the narrative now interrupted by history, the repressed—the feminine and the outcast—becomes first the voice of gentle Christianity but then suddenly evolves into its violent successor: the government colonizer with the gun. Violence and guns interrupt each part of the narrative: a gun accidentally kills Ezeudu's sixteen-year-old son in part 1, and violence deliberately destroys Abame in part 2. The ending descends on the reader as swiftly as the sudden (1900–06) arrival of the British and their control over Nigeria.

Things Fall Apart has a place in Nigeria's cultural heritage, and like all other objects of culture, it may be interrogated for what it contains, conceals, and depends on. As a novel written in the language of the oppressor, it is a "Whited Sepulchre" that, like Joseph Conrad's ivory, owes its prestige to its source in horror (Conrad 13). As Walter Benjamin reminds us, "There is no document of civilization which is not at the same time a document of barbarism" (258). As historically constructed forms, written literature in general and the African novel in particular, even as they forge new structures of defiance in new English languages and old African languages, acknowledge their roots in the writer's psyche colonized by other texts; in other forms of Western literature; in the colonization of Igbo by English, of Africa by the West; and in the insistent reflection and construction of conflicted and plural texts that simultaneously betray and realize the writer's ends. Like the hero he has chosen, Achebe defeats his own monologic and centripetal intent, although the monologic purpose might have worked had he been writing a poem. But because the novel is a decentralized, centrifugal, and dialogic genre, it works against the cultural norms of society rather than with them; Achebe's novel, therefore, works against what might have been his original intention and desire—the wish to celebrate the tribe's ideology and to commit what he calls "an act of atonement with my past, the ritual return and homage of a prodigal son" (*Morning* 70). The "mad logic of the Trinity" that seduces Nwoye becomes, as it were, the heart of whiteness of this novel, and it conducts a secret war with its masculine, tribal, and epic codes (104). The class admits its difficulties with the lyricism of the passages that describe the triumph of Christianity:

> It was the poetry of the new religion, something felt in the marrow. The hymn about brothers who sat in darkness and in fear seemed to answer a vague and persistent question that haunted his young soul —the question of the twins crying in the bush and the question of Ikemefuna who was killed. He felt a relief within as the hymn poured into his parched soul. The words of the hymn were like the drops of frozen rain melting on the dry palate of the panting earth.   (104)

Students confess to confusion as they side with and against the church that, because of its early support of weak outcasts and the wretched of the clan, prepared the way for colonial conquest. But when they also see how the presence of the slippery and unstable female code disturbs the unstable rigidity of masculine codes in all three sections of the novel, they begin to recognize dimensions of discord in the historical, mythic, and political unconscious of the novel. They understand (echoing the distinction between the oral and the written) that in the mythic mode the disturbance is circular—Okonkwo's crime against Ani is punished by exile and a return— but that in the historical mode the disturbance is linear, and Okonkwo's crime against the European is met by death.

As we end our discussion of this novel, I hope that my students have overcome their monologic resistance to its life, that they accept the novel as a necessarily messy and disappointing crucible of experience written by a man who is a product of a continuing history whose shape he is trying to change even as he rewrites it into fiction. Although *Things Fall Apart* is no nearer to monolithic "truth" about Africa or Africans than Joyce Cary's much vilified *Mister Johnson* is, it has brought us to a more pluralistic understanding of the modern African novel, of the problems inherent in decolonized discourse, and of Achebe's world. And my students are nearer to a more truthfully complex disappointment than they were when the class began.

NOTE

[1]I use the term *Third World* to denote the historical and political reality that subordinated, evaluated, and named colonized peoples; that associated value with industrialization; and that provided a linguistic and cultural site for a particular kind of multivoiced conflict.

Narrative, Metacommentary, and Politics in a "Simple" Story

Wahneema Lubiano

If, as Henry Louis Gates, Jr., argues, European and American critics have appropriated African literature as anthropological evidence about African culture (5), then within the terms of that appropriation the Western critical reception of Achebe's work has made consistent, if not imaginative, sense. Such critical response to Achebe's corpus has encouraged a perception of his early novels as "simple" works, a perception that strips those texts of self-conscious intention and refuses to acknowledge (or even see) the language manipulation that makes them artistic works instead of mere documentary evidence of the exotic "other."

My undergraduate students consistently respond to *Things Fall Apart* by insisting on the ethnographic value of Achebe's work. Students seem unwilling to apply to so different a text the literary tools they are learning to use with texts whose "realism" they recognize. Instead, they unself-consciously valorize what they see as the novel's cultural authenticity.

Strange indeed is this insistence on simplicity and anthropology in response to the wealth of cultural and ritual detail in Achebe's text, especially when critics celebrate the weighty details of nineteenth-century middle-class British decorum represented in George Eliot's *Middlemarch* or the drawing-room psychology of Henry James's novels. Gates's concern about the critical use of African (and African American) texts as unnuanced cultural ethnography speaks to the dilemma of many black writers and critics who argue that such use, deliberate or not, represses the structure and the form of black texts. This repression in turn assists students in their "lazy" (and culturally parochial) readings of those texts. Of far greater value to students is an exploration of the repressed form of the text.

In a class I taught at the University of Texas, Austin, entitled Black Modern and Postmodern Fiction, we focused on the representations of inside, or personal, consciousness and on the ways in which the narrative draws attention to the metacommentary individuals and groups use to intervene in and reconstruct reality. By metacommentary, I refer to the elaborated and explanatory language of the characters that goes on beyond the record of events that constitutes the language of the plot. That is, the characters not only generate narratives that make up the action of the text but consistently comment on one another's narratives in an interestingly complicated and transformative manner. In these terms, the reality of the group represented in *Things Fall Apart* flows along lines of convoluted narrative. In other words, the narrative laconically depicts a selection process but subtly hints at the power of narrative embedded in various speakers' storytelling and rhetoric. Although the story seems to pose as representation without mediation of the group's history of itself—without an omnipresent authorial commentary on the action—the text constantly shifts the responsibility for telling and interpreting from speaker to speaker. Reinterpretation becomes the means by which the narrative function is preempted and then co-opted by the most articulate members of an oral community.

Character in this text, therefore, is not a unified and stable identity always before us but a slippery ability (in the hands of various speakers) to renegotiate the terms of someone else's perception of reality or of oneself. Unoka, the village deadbeat, for example, snatches a moment in the midst of Okoye's just denunciation of his behavior to remake himself and the rationale for his actions. When Okoye, a "great talker," insists that Unoka repay the two hundred cowries that Okoye has loaned him, Unoka puts together a visual representation of the number of cowries that he owes various men:

> "Each group there represents a debt to someone, and each stroke is one hundred cowries. You see, I owe that man a thousand cowries. But he has not come to wake me up in the morning for it. I shall pay you, but not today. Our elders say that the sun will shine on those who stand before it shines on those who kneel under them. I shall pay my big debts first." . . . Okoye rolled his goatskin and departed.
>
> (6)

This language derails Okoye's narrative, which would have forced Unoka to repay the cowries and represented him as a character who avoids paying his debts, a bad man among men of good character. That Unoka had a bad reputation anyway is not as important as the way in which the text allows even Unoka to manipulate language to rewrite what is "really" happening and what is "really" known about him. Unoka's narrative forces Okoye, who had elaborately described his own version of history, to pick up his goatskin and leave—without his two hundred cowries. Unoka's rhetoric recodes the previous delineation of his character and disrupts the text's established limits on his power to describe his place in that community.

The text's representation of storytelling and the numerous references to proverbs and conversation both as art and as a way of life provide a metacommentary on the ability of language to construct a counternarrative that comments on, describes, and changes material reality. In one casual reference to the tribe's fear of darkness, for example, the text refers to the power of renaming: "A snake was never called by its name at night, because it would hear. It was called a string" (7). Thus, the snake loses the power to frighten. The text represents reality as a rhetorical triumph over facticity insofar as people empower themselves linguistically to negotiate the otherwise paralyzing fears of daily life.

As this buried play with language surfaces again and again, the narrative becomes a chronicle of a people who seem to live natural, unartificial lives but who distribute governing power according to an individual's rhetorical ability. In conversations and communal palavers, the most sophisticated speakers and rhetorical artificers provide the impetus for decisions and ensure the "reading" of reality that leads to action. Their interpretations, however, are continually open to disruption by more persuasive rhetoric.

The narrative deftly manipulates language relations to undermine the reader's expectation of a linear plot line. The beginning of the text, for example, tells us that Okonkwo "was well known" (3). The narrative evokes this entirely conventional and recognizable depiction of his personal history in terms of finite and human time: he brought honor to his village when he was eighteen by throwing the Cat, a wrestler unbeaten for seven years (3). But this recounting of personal and community history is casually yoked to mythic time at the end of the paragraph: "It was this man that Okonkwo threw in a fight which . . . was one of the fiercest since the founder of their town engaged a spirit of the wild for seven days and seven nights" (3).

Further, the narrative of the mythic fight has no real closure because the very next paragraph describes a fight scene that we cannot identify as Okonkwo's fight until the second sentence. The third paragraph has another time surprise for us: it tells us that Okonkwo's fight took place "many years ago, twenty years or more" (3), and we realize that we are back in the present waiting for present time history to continue.

The text telegraphs the importance of language even as it undermines our easy assumption that we are reading a simply told, straightforward narrative. Okonkwo, who is described in considerable physical detail, has a "slight stammer" and when angry cannot get his words out quickly enough (3). Again, the language of description is conventional enough, and Okonkwo is not so very different from any number of other less-than-articulate young men. The next paragraph, however, sets up the history of his father, a smooth talker indeed, and that history takes us back out of the present time and into the mists of the tribe's history. The text refuses both father and son a narrative or descriptive "ownership" of the relationship between them. It is not enough for the reader to see Okonkwo as the hard-working good seed that has fallen from the bad tree—Unoka—even if Okonkwo sees it that way. The "good" seed has a very "bad" problem within the constraints of this rhetorically driven community: he can't speak well enough to disrupt others' narratives or to consistently construct his own counternarrative; thus, he is forced to unambiguous and often deadly action.

These vacillations between Okonkwo's history and other micro- and macrohistories not only impede an unambiguously straightforward flow of narration but also reinforce, with constant narratives of rhetoric and oratory, the importance of language and storytelling to the life of the tribe. The narrative doubles back on itself so consistently that Okonkwo's story begins four different times, in four different places (chs. 1-4), and never in any kind of strict chronological order. In all these beginnings, the narrative unrelentingly insists on the importance of telling the tale, of getting back to the particular story of what happened as well as what happens generally (in proverbs). Each narrative focuses on the meaning of the story and, finally, includes an ongoing evaluation of how well the speaker has spoken. This community's day-to-day activities and metaphysics rely on narrative and metacommentary but not on a holistic and stable overall narrative. Is this "simple" storytelling?

The text ends with the threat of a new narrative from a narrator outside the community, the District Commissioner who plans to tell the tribe's story within the limits of a "reasonable" paragraph. But his narrative, *The Pacification of the Primitive Tribes of the Lower Niger*, is itself already undermined: that story has just been told.

While the traditional "histories" of European encounters with the dark other have written Africa for contemporary readers, this text, by historicizing and resetting the encounter in language from the other, fictionally anticipates the Commissioner's determination to write his own story. The already told story, all that precedes his meditation on his future writing project, not only disrupts the attempt to domesticate a brutal takeover of land, culture, and religion, it also deconstructs the Eurocentric gaze that defines the object, the other, as primitive.

I want to return finally to the pedagogical problem of teaching Achebe's tale to an audience predisposed, even educated, to read it only as ethnography and simple cultural representation of the exotic other. Cornel West, in a lecture at the University of Texas, Austin, asserted that the black body has "no public worth, only economic value as a laboring metabolism." I suggest that, within the terms of the world represented in *Things Fall Apart*, the black African body marks for the Commissioner and the missionaries the worth of their Christian, technological, and administrative triumph. But the narrative itself disrupts those triumphs even as it accurately recounts another historical "reality." It plays the double game that West calls the "African deification of accident—the sense of perennially being on a slippery tightrope." The narrative represents what he describes as the

> highly precarious historical situations in which black people have found themselves. . . . With political and economic avenues usually blocked, specific cultural arenas become the space wherein black resistance is channeled.

Ironically, this text engages in making tropes of the modern and postmodern. If modernism names narratives that describe a world altered by industry and technology in which mass destruction is not only possible but routine, if it names self-conscious skepticism about transcendent and empowering universal truths, then *Things Fall Apart* examines the narratives of political, economic, and military modernism that have destroyed the historical reality of a people. The novel is also postmodern, because it recognizes the problems of modernism and tries to address them. By reconstructing history and reality, the narrative resists the total obfuscation of the Igbo past. Caught in the postmodernist textual dilemma, *Things Fall Apart* rejects its own erasure even as it recasts colonialist history and refuses monolithic truth claims—a recasting and refusal exemplified by the constantly shifting interpretations of village palaver and proverbs.

Teaching the text in opposition to a simplistic, ethnographic reading of it disrupts the codifying effect of Eurocentric perception. Such pedagogy makes visible the artifice and self-willed intentionality of the text as a cultural object.

The Problem of Realism in *Things Fall Apart*: A Marxist Exegesis

Biodun Jeyifo

For my part, I make a systematic defense of the non-European civilizations. . . . They were communal societies, never societies of the many for the few. They were societies that were not only ante-capitalist, as has been said, but also anti-capitalist.

—Aimé Césaire

A people who free themselves from foreign domination will not be culturally free unless, without underestimating the importance of positive contributions from the oppressor's culture and other cultures, they return to the upwards paths of their own culture.

—Amilcar Cabral

As a contemporary classic, *Things Fall Apart* has dual acclaim. Not only is it the African novel of choice among the powerful guardians of literary taste in the First World, it is the only novel widely endorsed by most of the African cultural-literary intelligentsia, from conservative negritudist romancers of the African past to leftist dialecticians impatient with the romanticization of history.

What factors are responsible for the canonization of narratives like *Things Fall Apart* and Gabriel García Márquez's *One Hundred Years of Solitude*, not just as contemporary classics, but as texts that represent their respective regions of the world of letters? To what uses are such texts prone? The "momentous" events of literary history—even contemporary literary history—are not self-explanatory happenstances. Why, for instance, does *Things Fall Apart* enjoy much greater fame than Achebe's third novel, *Arrow of God*, a richer, more complex narrative? Furthermore, why do college teachers who place *Things Fall Apart* in course syllabi but who otherwise have no professional interest in African literature seldom go on to read *Arrow of God* or any other novel by Achebe? Although critics, teachers, and students applaud the memorableness, the "classical" simplicity, and the human interest of *Things Fall Apart*, these qualities can surely be found in many other African novels such as Ferdinand Oyono's *Old Man and the Medal* and Ngugi wa Thiong'o's *River Between* and *Weep Not, Child*.

These questions become even more pertinent when we consider that the status of *Things Fall Apart* as a double classic is regionally differentiated. Many Western critics and readers view the novel as an isolated African classic, though they sometimes regard Amos Tutuola's *Palm-Wine Drinkard* as a somewhat less than suitable companion to Achebe's novel. For African critics and readers, however, *Things Fall Apart* belongs in a nascent, expanding canonical firmament that includes narratives from writers like Ousmane Sembène, Ayi Kwei Armah, Mongo Beti, Tayeb Salih, Bessie Head, Mariama Bâ, and Nuruddin Farah.

The solid intertextuality of *Things Fall Apart*, evident when students read the novel along with *other* African contemporary classics, largely disappears when students read it apart from its African canonical context as Western practice often dictates. This practice replicates the center-periphery questions of unequal international economic and informational exchanges. Those in the center appropriate and abstract the cultural productions and realities of those on the periphery away from the periphery. Conversely, the periphery constructs its own canonical classics and enters the field through local or regional hegemonic discursive practice. Ngugi's recent creative and theoretical writings constitute a trenchant, eloquent critique of this point.

Teachers of *Things Fall Apart* may be unaware of their own hegemonic practices and discourses that promote the novel and other Third World texts as world classics abstracted from the literary traditions and the cultural and ideological milieus that produced them. The aesthetic and ideological features of realist fiction, however, seen in the light of the novel's status as a classic, ought to inform how we teach it. Realism, a justifiably dominant theme in the criticism and teaching of *Things Fall Apart*, has often been explored within the confines of either conscious or unwitting hegemonic discourse. Consequently, Achebe's realist intentions and achievements in the novel are abstracted from the historical dialectic that ought to inform a truly realist depiction of the past. This essay uses a deliberate, counterhegemonic approach to elaborate this subject. Marxism, with its extensive tradition of debates on realism, helps illuminate aspects of the narrative that are invisible to hegemonic discursive practice.

At the root of the novel's exceptional critical success is the consensus that the work maintains a rare, unsentimental, unvarnished realism. As a fictional mode, realism is more or less a spent force in Western literature, one assailed by high modernists, postmodernists, and radical-left avant-gardists. Its newly found creative and critical relevance in the colonial and postcolonial literature of Africa is a fascinating phenomenon of modern literary history that has received insufficient critical attention. While C. P. Snow needed a strenuous critical revisionism to celebrate the European and American realists in the midst of postmodernism, the myths and distortions of the vast colonialist literature on Africa made realism in the postcolonial context a historic and ideological necessity. The claims of authenticity in the colonial writer's image of Africa had never seriously entailed the rigorous realism that, since the publication of *Things Fall Apart*, has been invoked in relation to any writer's depiction of Africa. Indeed, the hegemonic Western critical orthodoxy of colonial writers like Joseph Conrad, Joyce Cary, and Graham Greene, along with popular romancers and lurid primitivists like Rider Haggard and Ann Mary Fielding, shifted critical discourse away from realist authenticity to constructs like psychosymbolism that effaced the continent, its peoples and cultures, and their full human worth. Only this critical sleight of hand, which made Africa a void, a mere symbolic construct in colonialist narratives of Africa, salvaged the seriousness and artistry of Conrad, Cary, and Greene from the embarrassing racism of their images of Africa and Africans.

In engaging the colonialist narrative tradition and carrying out a realist revolution, Achebe was very conscious of both the colonialist narratives and the hegemonic critical discourse that fed on them. The works of Conrad, Cary, and Greene were particularly important to Achebe (see "Image of Africa"). In his famous essay "The Novelist as Teacher," Achebe writes:

> I would be quite satisfied if my novels (especially the ones I set in the past) did no more than teach my readers that their past—with all its imperfections—was not one long night of savagery from which the first Europeans acting on God's behalf saved them.   (*Morning* 45)

As many theorists of realism have observed, the problem with realism is that it claims to be the mode of fiction closest to truth. Even though realism, with its plain narrative style and its "ethical" reserve about authorial omniscience, seems to possess an advantage over other modes, questions always remain about whose version of truth any narrative, realist or otherwise, proffers. Thus, while Achebe replaces colonial "Africans" like Joyce Cary's Mister Johnson or Conrad's riverboat cannibal in *Heart of Darkness* with realistic, named characters, he admits that realism is not an end in itself. In other words, Achebe's realist intentions hinge on *his* vision of truth, and that truth involves a partisan commitment to his African readers. As James Booth writes:

> Achebe sees his purpose in this novel as twofold. Firstly, it is an attempt . . . at "cultural retrieval," aimed at rescuing his traditional culture from the myths and distortions of the colonialist. . . . On the other hand he is aware of the equally dangerous myths and distortions which such a commitment may entail. . . . It is equally part of his purpose to avoid irresponsible idealisation. . . . Achebe then must steer a stylistic middle course between the Scylla of Conrad and Rider Haggard. . . . and the Charybdis of idealisation, which does perhaps threaten the work of other Nigerian writers such as Elechi Amadi and Flora Nwapa. . . . It is here that Achebe's skill in handling "clean" English, and his stylistic restraint stand him in good stead. . . . [Achebe's] even-paced narrative medium can . . . relate the less acceptable aspects of

traditional custom which are generally omitted from or subtly excused in the works of Amadi and Nwapa, without introducing the lurid emotionalism of Conrad's and other European views of Africa. The style possesses a dispassionateness which neither condemns nor attempts to excuse.   (79–81)

Critics often assert that, in spite of Achebe's authorial intentions, *Things Fall Apart* refurbishes the two putative central features of realist fiction—stylistic moderation and ideological objectivity. But the novel's resolution of the problem of realism is more apparent than real. Because the novel is "set in the past," Achebe cannot "objectively" avoid interpreting that past, especially when it involves crucial historical phenomena like colonization and the shift from precolonial culture to colonial capitalism. For Georg Lukács, neither "reportage" nor "portrayal," the two main variants of realism, can escape historical and ideological interpretation (*Essays* 45–75).

Emmanuel Ngara demonstrates in his book *Art and Ideology in the African Novel* that even a Marxist critic can flounder on Achebe's supposed objectivity. On the one hand, Ngara praises Achebe for his objectivity:

> In depicting the disintegration of Igbo culture in both *Things Fall Apart* and *Arrow of God* Achebe does not give us a partial or biased view of the historical epoch he is dealing with. . . . Thus we are able to see how political, religious, tribal and personal factors all contributed to the crumbling of the traditional social structure. . . . The author consequently succeeds in presenting a truthful and balanced account of reality and is able to capture the mood of the epoch. His method is that of objective realism.   (111–12)

But, on the other hand, Ngara argues that Achebe "does not present a Marxist or in any way radical view of social problems," and, consequently, his "art becomes a model of the triumph of realism over the claims of nationalism" (112).

A Marxist perspective that is not overly hasty in invoking concepts of socialist realism rejects the dominant "objectivity" view of Achebe's realism as abstract and somewhat reified. This dominant view, from such an undogmatic Marxist perspective, too easily reduces Achebe's realism to a mere balancing act in which he reconciles his commitment to portraying a past free of colonialist distortions and denigrations with an impartiality that "neither condemns nor attempts to excuse."

From such a critical Marxist perspective, the great triumph of Achebe's realism in *Things Fall Apart* is that the characters, situations, and feelings seem so concrete and memorable that social and human conflicts assume a logic of their own, quite independent of any abstract balancing act by the author in the service of objectivity. Friedrich Engels, in a letter that has become a central Marxist document on realism, explains how this inner logic of realism, this internal dialectic, springs directly from the narrative itself:

> I am far from finding fault with your not having written a point-blank socialist novel, a *"Tendenzroman"* as we Germans call it, to glorify the social and political views of the authors. That is not at all what I mean. The more the opinions of the author remain hidden, the better for the work of art. The realism I allude to may crop out even in spite of the author's opinions.   (803)

In his own way, and using completely different conceptions and imagery, Achebe expresses his predilection for this internal dialectic at the heart of reality:

> There is a dimension to things which I don't know exactly how to explain. And that's what you might call the unintended. I've used the phrase *powers of event* in *Arrow of God* when the *powers of event* achieve their own logic. For instance, you've already worked out things in considerable detail and you expect this to happen and that to happen, and then suddenly these things don't happen as you planned them. Something else, the unforeseen, chance, whatever it is, intervenes.
> (Qtd. in Jeyifo 12)

Although Achebe invokes concepts like the "unforeseen" and "chance," his deployment of the dialectic in the narrative of *Things Fall Apart* is anything but Hegelian; no abstract universal spirit using mere human agents as vehicles for its self-actualization stalks the characters and situations of this novel. The first part of the novel, in which Achebe describes the precolonial, precapitalist African village society in a manner so totalized it would meet Lukács's rigorous standards, illustrates this point. But Achebe provides more than the internal weaknesses of the precolonial village society; he offers extensive portraits of dominated and marginalized groups and individuals who later become the first converts to Christianity, the first functionaries of the new power structure and relations introduced by colonialism. Achebe renders the anguish and disaffection of these people—women, slaves, outcasts, Okonkwo's son Nwoye—with poignancy and solicitude more powerful than any revolutionary tract or pamphlet.

Achebe's unforced depiction of this dialectic achieves perhaps its greatest textual richness in the encounters between colonizer and colonized in the second half of the narrative. Individuals and groups become more insistent on their objectives and perceptions, and they act more decisively and tragically on these objectives and perceptions. At the same time, however, new, unintended processes and relations form that the characters perceive only dimly. The colonizers' coming, for instance, liberates the marginalized and powerless of the old order, but the new order introduces its own oppressions and alienations. The intolerant missionary, Mr. Smith, who succeeds the gentler, more understanding Mr. Brown; Enoch, an overzealous convert who uses his awareness of the secular power behind Christian evangelization to trample native traditions and sensibilities; the native functionaries of the colonial administration who wreak gratuitous humiliations on the most respected leaders of the colonized community—all are harbingers of the oppression the new order will superimpose on the restitution felt by the malcontents of the old order.

A tantalizing question remains: What if the colonizers had not come? Was the precolonial social order so static that its internal dialectic could not have found its own synthesis, its own resolution? That is, would people like Ikemefuna and Nwoye, the women subjected to the harsh patriarchal order or forced to cast away their twin children, or the despised *osu* have received restitution without colonialism? If we accept Amilcar Cabral's revolutionary dictum that postcolonial societies "must return to the upwards paths of their own culture" (*Unity* 143), what such paths are indicated in the dialectic of Achebe's narrative? Again, Engels's theory of realism is helpful:

> I think however that the solution of the problem must become manifest from the situation and the action themselves without being expressly pointed out and that the author is not obliged to serve the reader on a platter the future historical resolution of the social conflicts which he describes. (802)

In addition to the disaffected and marginalized of Umuofia, Achebe's novel includes moral reformers and dissenters like Obierika and Ogbuefi Ezeudu. Before Ikemefuna's killing, Ogbuefi Ezeudu warns Okonkwo: "That boy calls you father. Do not bear a hand in his death" (40). Could not these two different currents within the precolonial dialectic have eventually coalesced into a powerful river of transformation? Could change have come to Igboland without things falling apart? A history without colonization would have yielded a different "invisible" narrative, a different sort of representative text for Africa.

SPECIFIC COURSES

Teaching *Things Fall Apart* in the Humanities Core Course

Eric Sellin

Many humanities core courses, once limited to the study of the art and literature of the so-called Western world, today require professors to teach some non-Western culture. For various reasons—demographic, bibliographical, and aesthetic—African culture is often deemed the most appropriate culture to study.

In establishing the basic reading list for any period or movement, teachers must make difficult choices. For example, should one teach John Locke's *Second Treatise of Government* or Jean-Jacques Rousseau's *Social Contract*? Both illustrate the intellectual ambience of the seventeenth and eighteenth centuries that fostered the ideas and discourse of the Declaration of Independence. The canon of African readings is subject to similar debates.

First, should students read literature by Africans written in the colonizer's language? Some critics contend that such writing, aimed—as it is bound to be—at markets in Europe, reinforces and perpetuates the attitudes and prejudices resulting from colonization. At the level of culture assimilation one can reasonably expect in a freshman core course, however, teachers are unlikely to see any profound difference between an "ethnographic" English-language novel like Achebe's *Things Fall Apart* (or its French-language counterpart, Camara Laye's *L'enfant noir*) and a translation from an oral or written account in an African language. One can even argue that African literature written in a European language at least has an African "translating" the cultural experience behind the narrative into the European idiom. No doubt the questions of what should constitute the African literary canon and who should interpret that literature are valid ones; but these questions have little practical importance in a discussion of the problems and methods involved in introducing uninitiated readers to African culture. For relatively uninitiated instructors teaching core courses whose syllabi are principally devoted to other areas, this task can be complex.

Several pitfalls are inherent in Western civilization or humanities core courses, which, by definition, range across the centuries and the continents. Problems occur whenever a program features abrupt transitions, even in courses limited to one cultural tradition. The introduction of extreme cultural differences naturally magnifies any such difficulty.

I have frequently taught a freshman core course called Intellectual Heritage, in which we devote fifteen to twenty percent of the semester to a Third World culture. The course leaps, perforce, from topic to topic: from Romantic poetry to Einstein, from *Gilgamesh* to Aeschylus, from Marx to cubism, and so forth. Generally, my examinations for this course include a series of brief identification questions based on the lectures and discussions and on the assigned readings. I have collected some "gems" on the identification section of my examination. One student explained that "anapest" (the metrical foot) was "a nineteenth-century socialist utopian" and, closer to home, another student defined "muons" (the short-lived atomic subparticles) as "African finger foods or children's toys described in *Things Fall Apart*." In short, students in a core-curriculum course sometimes write amusingly absurd answers on examinations whether they are questioned on *Oedipus the King*, Genesis, *The Origin of Species*, or *Things Fall Apart*.

The misunderstandings entailed by abrupt transitions from Newton to Romanticism, for example, usually disappear as students move through their undergraduate careers. For some students, however, the core-curriculum introduction to a Third World culture—such as the African—may be their only formal academic exposure to that culture. Thus, teachers of that culture should strive to make the material self-sufficient, self-sustaining, and meaningful. Of course, a Third World topic that seems arbitrary and bewildering to the unapprised student may also prove bewildering to the nonspecialist instructor who is probably at least vaguely familiar with all the Western civilization topics on the core syllabus.

Of the dozen or so novels that provide suitable insight into the traditional African ethos, an African specialist can choose the work that best conveys his or her understanding of African culture. The nonspecialist teacher of a core-curriculum course must depend on outside advice. *Things Fall Apart* is not a difficult text like, say, *Nedjma* by the Algerian writer Kateb Yacine, but problems can arise if teachers do not adequately prepare their students.

Even without any special knowledge of Africa, the average student readily appreciates many features of *Things Fall Apart*, including the novel's limpid style, its lyrical descriptions of nature, its swift-moving narrative action, its informational and documentary interest, its convincing use of dialogue, and its occasional humorous moments. But the novel can also provide a window on another culture if students become active, emotional learners rather than passive recipients of information. Ancillary lectures and readings can help instructors achieve this goal.

Ideally, teachers should "situate" the book in a historical and emotional context; I have found it possible to do this without devoting an entire semester to the study of Africa. I suggest the following syllabus, which assumes four to eight hours of instruction in a typical Monday-Wednesday-Friday class, for nonspecialist teachers of *Things Fall Apart*.

First Week

Monday: Lecture on the colonization of Africa (part 1). This subject is tremendously vast and complex, but, with a few reference books, the teacher can prepare a compact lecture reviewing Africa's colonial history, from the Portuguese coastal activity of the mid-1400s to the Berlin conference of 1884–85 to twentieth-century corporate development. Instructors should have students read, by Friday's class, chapters 4, 6, and 8 of Colin Turnbull's *Lonely African*, which may be placed on reserve in the library.

Wednesday: Lecture on the colonization of Africa (part 2). In this lecture and subsequent discussion, the class explores in some depth the economic, military, and religious penetration of Africa. Students should read excerpts from "The Communist Manifesto" and other texts involving colonialism, and the instructor's lecture should include a concise economic profile of colonialism as an outgrowth of the Industrial Revolution and as a phenomenon in symbiosis with the events of that period.

Friday: Discussion session on Ibrahimo in Turnbull's Lonely African *(chapters 4, 6, and 8).* This reading assignment has, in my experience, never failed to elicit an extreme reaction from the students. The three chapters describe how Ibrahimo—a young African boy at a mission school who wishes to go through the circumcision ceremony with his age group—is tricked by a missionary and preemptively circumcised at the mission hospital so that he cannot participate in the "evil" native ceremony. Ibrahimo laments that he can never, thereafter, be a "man" among his people, and yet he grows up to realize that he has not achieved equality with the Europeans either.

The arrogance of the missionary's presumptuous deed invariably infuriates my students. This reading assignment produces lively, sometimes controversial discussion; creates empathy with the African; and serves as a documentary backdrop for some of the episodes involving Europeans in *Things Fall Apart*.

Second Week

Monday: Decolonization in Africa. This lecture deals with the major events of the twentieth century that led up to the wave of revolutions and independence movements in the Third World—with special focus on Africa from 1940 to the present. The lecture should also address the psychology of the colonizer and the colonized, summarizing for students the concepts popularized in Albert Memmi's *Colonizer and the Colonized* and Frantz Fanon's *Wretched of the Earth.* At the end of class, teachers might conduct a discussion on a single far-reaching subject: Why would the leader of an African independence movement turn to Marxist-Leninist writings when formulating the program for a new society? In my core-program class, the students have already seen that Jefferson, in drafting the Declaration of Independence, favored accepted British and Continental models of thought that nonetheless seemed to accommodate the revolutionaries' activities. The students are thus prepared to see, by analogy, that the Africans would naturally lean toward political theorists—such as Marx, Engels, and Lenin—who specifically took into account the colonial situation. I try to convey to students, in this way, that the dynamics of African Marxism are quite distinct from those of contemporary European Marxism. This issue, which usually provokes constructive disagreement and discussion, also generates good essay questions for midterm and final examinations, as well as topics for student papers.

Wednesday: Discussion of Things Fall Apart. Students should have finished the book by this class meeting. Teachers may devote this session to discussing the novel on a rather superficial level (with appropriate blackboard reinforcement) and to reviewing the following topics:

the names of the principal characters
the basic plot
characterization
the portrayal of good and evil
the literary style
descriptions of nature
use of the proverb, that African repository of wisdom and tradition, as a
    prime exponent of discourse
humor, with special attention to the "your buttocks" and "ashy buttocks"
    interpreter episodes in the book

Instructors should begin with very simple questions (such as asking students who the characters are) and then move on to somewhat less obvious details (such as showing on the map where the action occurs and discussing the living conditions, the weather, and the landscape of the area as Achebe reports them). Class discussion finally turns to more abstract functions (such as listing the good and evil traits in characters and actions), though I prefer to save most such challenging topics for the next class meeting.

Friday: Discussion of Things Fall Apart *(continued).* In this session, the discussion focuses on more subtle and complex tasks, such as linking *Things Fall Apart* with the Turnbull reading and with the earlier lectures on colonization and decolonization. Discussion topics might include traditionalism versus modernism, the existence of evil in traditional society as Achebe describes it, the reasons the old society falls apart, and the society's ability to recover the old once the new has had an effect. If the core course has already covered Greek tragedy, other appropriate discussion topics might involve *hubris* and Okonkwo as a tragic figure in the classical sense and whether we can, or should, explicate an African work like *Things Fall Apart* in terms of Western models.

Instructors may put two interesting support documents on reserve in the library and ask students to read them for this class session. Chapter 3 of *Ambiguous Adventure (L'aventure ambiguë)* by the Senegalese author Cheikh Hamidou Kane, weighs the merits of fighting colonialism by maintaining traditional values against those of adopting the new ways in order to combat the interlopers more successfully. *No Longer at Ease*, Achebe's disturbing sequel to *Things Fall Apart*, shows the moral corruption and thievery that result from the loss of the old society and the establishment of sprawling colonial cities like Lagos.

Should the semester's syllabus permit the allocation of one or two more class days to this unit, teachers might use the extra time to discuss *No Longer at Ease* more fully or to show the 1973 film version of *Things Fall Apart*, which incorporates both that novel and *No Longer at Ease*. (For a detailed description of this film, see Larson, "Film.") Another, more recent film version of *Things Fall Apart* exists, but because it consists of thirteen, one-hour episodes it is inappropriate for classroom adoption, unless the teacher wishes to show students a single episode (several people have recommended episode 8) for entertainment purposes or for cultural orientation.

Finally, instructors might find two other books useful as further reading for honors students. Alan Moorehead's *Fatal Impact* chronicles culture contact and contamination in the South Pacific in the days of James Cook, Louis Antoine de Bougainville, and others. Along with *Things Fall Apart* and *No Longer at Ease*, Achebe's fourth novel, *A Man of the People*, brilliantly captures the decline of traditional values and the spread of moral decay in modern Africa, the blame for which many people categorically attribute to the colonial adventure.

Teaching *Things Fall Apart* in a Criticism Course

Richard K. Priebe

A few years ago I started using *Things Fall Apart* in a practical criticism course and found it an ideal text to help students understand social and historical approaches to literature. My choice of any text for this course depends on whether it effectively demonstrates the applications of literary criticism and answers the practical demands of undergraduate writers. As the scholarship on *Things Fall Apart* indicates, the novel invites a variety of critical approaches, but I have used it only to teach the social and historical perspectives. English majors take the course, Approaches to Literature, in their junior year as one of their first major courses. It is not, however, a required course, and it tends to draw an almost equal number of nonmajors. It aims to show students that appreciating and understanding a text are connected to the ways we talk and write about it. As a practical course, my class contains little history or theory of criticism. To establish a common body of texts, I select the same kinds of primary texts used in introduction to literature courses—a general anthology (poetry, short fiction, and drama) and two novels. I start with the formalist approach and then move to the historical, sociological, biographical, and psychological, giving a nod to reader response, deconstruction, and other postmodernist theories. I assign one or two key articles that illustrate or discuss a given approach and then flesh out the details of the approach through lecture and discussion focused on a specific text. Along the way, the students write four essays employing the various approaches and a critical review of a work of criticism or theory.

My students are diverse—old and young, full-time and working, experienced readers and neophytes, some with many literature courses behind them, others with none. While these factors may be specific to the urban university I teach in, they generally reflect demographic and curricular changes common to most American universities. Teachers familiar with a course like the one I outline may be skeptical of New Criticism, but they know they must emphasize close reading. They also know that, after some rapid progress, they must make the jump from isolated text to the text in the web of social and historical formations. As Harry Levin once pointed out, we want our discerners to be learners and our close readers to move to scholarship (205), but no one, including Levin, has ever shown how we can teach the learning requisite for clear discerning. Despite our skepticism that we must "cheat" to supply "background," we know background cannot be neatly packaged.

On a theoretical level, students readily accept the importance of contextual material, but they just as readily resist putting theory into practice, particularly if the teacher asks them to find significant material as well as to apply it in a meaningful analysis. Students usually follow what the teacher has to say about a sociological analysis of a text—teachers are supposed to give them such information. But students may find that applying the lesson in their own essays is overwhelming. In addition, the more familiar the text, the more application creates a problem. American students assume they already know most of the contextual information about an American novel. They might see some strange new cultural or historical details, but they generally feel they can work these out (or dismiss them) as oddities of the text, of culture, or of history. *Things Fall Apart*, especially when paired with E. L. Doctorow's *Ragtime* or Theodore Dreiser's *Sister Carrie*, can make the strange familiar and enable students to make the familiar strange, so that at last they arrive at a new familiarity.

Admittedly, sociological and historical criticism covers material and positions that are often at odds. While I do not avoid issues of theory, I keep my central aims both limited and practical. The major goal is to expand student awareness of the text-context relation, and here *Things Fall Apart* works well because it is far removed from any context American students think they know. Though the text is clearly not inaccessible without outside help, almost every detail calls for additional contextual clarification. One of the wonders of this work is that Achebe takes great care in explaining cultural terms, beliefs, and so on. His realism makes the work seem artless and transparent, but the more one knows about Igbo life, the more richly complex the novel becomes.

Students generally have little trouble seeing that a literary work is also a historical document, but that perception can cause them problems when they first attempt historical criticism. Some students go to history texts to verify elements in the literary text; others simply reverse the process. Investigating historical-literary connections any other way looks confusing if not overwhelming. Students need to learn that the connections may not be obvious but also that the complexity need not be confusing. As I talk about *Things Fall Apart*, I ask my students to consider two points. First, although the novel is about one historical period, the 1890s, it was written in another, the 1950s. Much can be done with this basic observation, but essentially I want the students to realize that they do not necessarily need to consult histories of the early colonial period in Nigeria. The novel is a document from the end of the colonial era, and we may find some more immediately enlightening material if we examine the context of political and cultural nationalism in which Achebe wrote it. For teachers, this activity involves little more than presenting background, though I like to focus on specific connections between that historic moment and the novel's didactic thrust, its metahistorical content, and even its linguistic structure (since Achebe chose to write in English and not in Igbo).

Second, I have my students examine the seemingly discrete cultural terms and concepts they believe I must define before they can fully understand the text. Any class discussion of this text typically begins with a barrage of questions—about kola, yam, palm-wine, *chi, ogbanje*, and so on. Next come questions about broader issues of religion, folklore, colonialism, kinship structure, and agriculture, but I defer most of these issues until later. I do answer some questions, but most I turn back to the students, for *Things Fall Apart* enables them to become more immediately involved with historical-sociological criticism, with less confusing results, than is possible with a novel closer to home. I give them one or two brief excerpts from Victor Uchendu's *Igbo of Southeast Nigeria* and Achebe's *Morning Yet on Creation Day* and have them work together in small discussion groups to discuss how the material sheds light on the novel. Uchendu's descriptions of oracles, ancestors, and kola hospitality and Achebe's essay "Chi in Igbo Cosmology" are excellent. Most groups easily find two or three ways these pieces enhance our understanding of the novel.

It usually takes a week to work through these exercises and general discussion. I then spend a second week explaining to students how to find relevant social and historical information and showing them how they might use that information in discussing the text. Here the most difficult aspect of teaching historical criticism arises. If the teacher allows students to use the library to do original research, they easily discover C. L. Innes and Bernth Lindfors's *Critical Perspectives on Chinua Achebe* and Robert M. Wren's *Achebe's World*, both of which contain enough material to fill many solid research papers with information other scholars have gathered. But such an exercise is often as boring to the teacher who has to read the paper as it is to the student who has to write it; moreover, the pedagogical value is very limited. If the students cannot do the original research, they should at least understand the process. Later, when they work on the American novel, they may use the library, but for now I keep them away from it. By the end of the first week, they have raised a number of significant questions about the text that demand a social or historical response. I work as a resource person, providing the material they need.

In particular, two questions that are bound to come up provide the focus for the entire week. First, students want to know if the novel is "true" in that limited historical sense of whether the characters existed and the events took place. Second, they want to learn more about male and female roles in Igbo society and to know whether that information might help them understand the many ways the novel emphasizes gender. These questions point to two basic ways the historical-cultural approach helps explain a text: it teaches us about sources or influences and it reveals the encoded values.

Though the first question—whether the novel is "true"—has a simple answer, I hesitate to give it. Finding one-to-one correspondences is a relatively minor aspect of exploring sources and influences, and I want the students to look broadly across society as well as specifically at historical events (i.e., horizontally as well as vertically, ethnographically as well as historically). I talk about some of the fictionalized history Wren discusses, especially Obierika's account of the white man with a bicycle who is killed in Abame (*Achebe's World* 26–31), and point out the range of sources Wren drew on: colonial archives, local tradition, and history texts. We investigate the extent to which Achebe uses virtually every aspect of traditional Igbo life, especially Igbo oral art. (Before we start with Achebe, we consider the question of sources and influences for some poems by Yeats and Auden, so the students understand when I raise this issue again in relation to Achebe.) I mention Achebe's borrowing from Yeats and his more subtle and negative debt to Joyce Cary, but I caution that Achebe's anonymous traditional sources are richer still. Sometimes students who have had a course in folklore make helpful comments, though most students have no idea where one might find those sources or why anyone might want them. I always have to point out the obvious, that unless we look outside the text we cannot know if Achebe has incorporated traditional material and that once we know where and how he has used such sources, we are in a better position to appreciate the novel as a whole. I bring in collections of folktales and proverbs, as well as standard reference works such as *The Types of the Folktale* (Aarne and Thompson), to show students how to find sources that are clearly not as fixed as written texts. Versions of the tale about the conflict between heaven and earth and the tale about the greedy tortoise named "All of you" are common throughout West Africa, and though it is never possible to find the definitive source, students see how directly Achebe has drawn from his culture. They begin to recognize, as they later discover in relation to the American novel, that a story's art often has more to do with the ways a writer uses cultural material than with the pure invention of material. Here, of course, I want the students to consider Achebe's use of folk material in developing theme, symbolic structure, and plot (see, e.g., Weinstock and Ramadan).

I always conclude the section on Achebe by explaining that almost any judicious examination of the cultural material a writer includes can illuminate the values embedded in a text. Lindfors's article on Achebe's use of proverbs is an excellent example of this type of research ("Palm-Oil"), but I also draw on my own work to show that the proverbs establish a strategy for the novel as a whole (*Myth*). Just as a proverb clarifies a particular social situation, this novel functions as a proverb that clarifies a particular historical moment of a particular people. We end, however, by returning to the question of gender and its cultural significance. The conflict between values the novel represents as male and female is so basic to the narrative structure that no serious discussion can avoid it. Obviously, Okonkwo's rejection of all that is female defines virtually everything he does, but the polarized values appear in more subtle ways in the novel's tales, rituals, deities, objects, and activities. Students see that culturally valorized elements are often connected in significant patterns. In a text that initially seems different if not strange, students easily recognize individual cultural elements; the cultural and historical approach helps them appreciate these larger patterns.

With more familiar texts, students have trouble even identifying historical or cultural elements, and writing critically about those elements can be a challenging experience. The less familiar the culture, the more likely we are to think of its texts as full of cultural elements to the exclusion of any art (see, e.g., almost any early review of an Achebe novel by a Western critic); the more familiar the text, the more likely its cultural elements will seem transparent. The "exotic" text shows students that everything in a text is indeed historical and cultural, though they must learn that their sense of the exotic has to do with their limited point of view. That lesson learned, students are better able to approach a text in their own culture from a social-historical perspective. I try to choose texts, such as *Ragtime* and *Sister Carrie*, that have an abundance of accessible primary cultural data.

I ask the students to choose topics to write on, and a little class discussion of either novel in relation to Achebe's work starts generating those topics. I want them to see the familiar as strange; *Ragtime* suggests two starting points. The story takes place in the New York area at the turn of the century and focuses on the lives of three fictional families—a middle-class white family, an immigrant Jewish family, and a black family—whose paths cross and sometimes connect with famous historical individuals such as Henry Ford, Harry Houdini, J. P. Morgan, Emma Goldman, and Robert Peary. Having looked at Igbo society through Achebe, students are curious about the accuracy of *Ragtime* as an ethnography and the extent to which it treats family structure, male and female roles, ethnicity, class, and so on in a full and representative manner. Students also ask the same fundamental historical question that they did with Achebe—Is the story true? While some scenes and events are too bizarre to have ever happened, fiction keeps sliding into fact. Other points of comparison also arise: Why do both Achebe and Doctorow write about the turn of the century? To what extent is Doctorow, like Achebe, making a social comment on the present? Regardless of the specific topic students choose, they often find it useful to keep these questions in mind as they start their research.

When I teach *Ragtime*, I arrange time to work with the students in the library. For the most part, they ferret out relevant social and historical books on their own, but they need some guidance in locating the highly useful material in old newspapers and magazines on microfilm and microfiche. Their papers sometimes turn out overly general or mechanical, but a surprising number of students find source materials like those Doctorow drew on (especially in the *New York Times* and *National Geographic*), and they often make sharp comments on how he included such material.

The critical edition of *Sister Carrie* makes that novel easier to work with since it contains some of the material Dreiser used in creating his own characters and story. The drawback, of course, is that students never get the experience of "discovering" this material for themselves. I usually encourage students who write about *Sister Carrie* to analyze what the material clarifies in the text. While the best papers on *Ragtime* focus on the source material, the best papers on this novel typically explore social institutions and conditions or the novel's moral vision in relation to the standards of the time. The popularity of gender-related topics makes discussions pertaining to gender (vis-à-vis the author, the characters, and the social institutions in which they move) quite useful.

It might be instructive to reverse this process in an African university and teach the social-historical approach by starting with an American novel and then moving to an African work. I have not had the chance to try such an experiment, though when I taught American literature at a Ghanaian university, I found I had to take the same kind of social-historical approach in presenting American novels as I do in teaching *Things Fall Apart* to American students. In a certain sense, I discovered the obvious, but even with the Ghanaian emphasis on approaching texts sociologically and historically, the experience confirmed my sense that my criticism students at home have much to gain by studying Achebe's novel.

CONTRIBUTORS AND SURVEY PARTICIPANTS

The editor thanks the following scholars and teachers of African literature, whose generous help and support made this volume possible.

Chinua Achebe, Nsukka, Nigeria; Edna Aizenberg, Marymount Manhattan College; E. Curtis Alexander, Chesapeake, VA; Kwaku Amoabeng, Paterson, NJ; Lauri Anderson, Suomi College; Stephen H. Arnold, University of Alberta; Rebecca A. Bodenner, Temple University; Susan Broadhead, University of Louisville; Sarah Brown-Clark, Youngstown State University; Robert Cancel, University of California, San Diego; Mary M. Cermak, University of the District of Columbia; Ernest Champion, Bowling Green State University; Rhonda Cobham, Amherst College; Greta Coger, Northwest Mississippi Junior College; Arlene A. Elder, University of Cincinnati; Ernest Emenyonu, University of Calabar, Nigeria; J. Randolph Fisher, Savannah State College; Simon Gikandi, University of Michigan; Irene C. Goldman, Ball State University; Georg M. Gugelberger, University of California, Riverside; Lee Haring, Brooklyn College; Barbara Harlow, University of Texas, Austin; Hunt Hawkins, Florida State University; Mildred Hill-Lubin, University of Florida; Lisa Iyer, University of California, Riverside; Dan Izevbaye, University of Ibadan, Nigeria; Biodun Jeyifo, Cornell University; Rotimi Johnson, Lagos State University, Nigeria; Feroza Jussawalla, University of Texas, El Paso; G. D. Killam, University of Guelph; Bruce King, Muncie, IN; Viney Kirpal, Indian Institute of Technology, Bombay; Edward C. Knox, Middlebury College; George Lang, University of Alberta; Carrol Lasker, State University of New York, Stony Brook; Bernth Lindfors, University of Texas, Austin; Wahneema Lubiano, Princeton University; Jack Mapanje, Chancellor College, University of Malawi; Mildred Mortimer, University of Colorado, Boulder; Sister Mary Henry Nachtsheim, The College of St. Catherine; Ashton Nichols, Dickinson College; J. O. J. Nwachukwu-Agbada, Anambra State College of Education, Awka, Nigeria; Christopher S. Nwodo, University of Port Harcourt, Nigeria; Donatus Nwoga, University of Nigeria, Nsukka; Emmanuel Obiechina, Hobart and William Smith Colleges; Augustine Okereke, Anambra State College of Education, Awka, Nigeria; E. Imafedia Okhamafe, University of Nebraska, Omaha; Philip O'Mara, Jackson State University; Damian Opata, University of Nigeria, Nsukka; Richard K. Priebe, Virginia Commonwealth University; Eric Sellin, Tulane University; Jay Silverman, Nassau Community College; Zohreh T. Sullivan, University of Illinois, Urbana; Michael Thelwell, University of Massachusetts, Amherst; Pearl Thomas, Orange Coast College and University of California, Irvine; Ousseynou B. Traoré, Cleveland State University; Maureen Warner-Lewis, University of the West Indies, Kingston; Mark A. Weinstein, University of Nevada, Las Vegas; Robert M. Wren, University of Houston.

WORKS CITED

Aarne, Antti, and Stith Thompson. *The Types of the Folktale*. Helsinki: Academia Scientiarum Fennica, 1928.

Abraham, W. E. *The Mind of Africa*. Chicago: U of Chicago P, 1963.

Abrahams, Cecil A. "George Lamming and Chinua Achebe: Tradition and the Literary Chroniclers." *Awakened Conscience: Studies in Commonwealth Literature*. Ed. C. D. Narasimhaiah. New Delhi: Sterling, 1978. 294–306.

———. "Margaret Laurence and Chinua Achebe: Commonwealth Storytellers." *ACLALS Bulletin* 5.3 (1980): 74–85.

Achebe, Chinua. "The African Writer and the Biafran Cause." *Kroniek van Afrika* 8 (1968): 65–70; *Conch* 1.1 (1969): 8–14. Rpt. in Achebe, *Morning* 78–84.

———. "The African Writer and the English Language." *Moderna Språk* 58 (1964): 438–46; *Transition* 18 (1965): 27–30. Rpt. in Achebe, *Morning* 55–62.

———. *Anthills of the Savannah*. London: Heinemann, 1987.

———. *Arrow of God*. London: Heinemann, 1964.

———. "The Black Writer's Burden." *Présence africaine* 59 (1966): 135–40.

———. "Chi in Igbo Cosmology." Achebe, *Morning* 93–103.

———. Foreword. *African Prose I: Traditional Oral Texts*. Ed. W. H. Whiteley. London: Clarendon, 1964. vii–xi.

———. *Hopes and Impediments: Selected Essays, 1965–87*. London: Heinemann, 1988.

———. "An Image of Africa." *Massachusetts Review* 18 (1977): 782–94.

———. "Language and the Destiny of Man." Achebe, *Morning* 30–37.

———. *A Man of the People*. London: Heinemann, 1966.

———. *Morning Yet on Creation Day: Essays*. London: Heinemann, 1975.

———. "Named for Victoria, Queen of England." *New Letters* 40.1 (1973): 15–22. Rpt. in Achebe, *Morning* 65–70; Achebe, *Hopes* 20–26.

———. *No Longer at Ease*. London: Heinemann, 1960.

———. "The Novelist as Teacher." *New Statesman* 29 Jan. 1965: 161–62. Rpt. in Achebe, *Morning* 42–45; Achebe, *Hopes* 27–31.

———. "The Role of the Writer in a New Nation." Killam, *African Writers* 7–13.

———. *Things Fall Apart*. African Writers Series. London: Heinemann Educational, 1962; 1988.

———. *Things Fall Apart*. London: Heinemann, 1958.

———. *Things Fall Apart*. New York: Astor-Honor, 1959.

———. *Things Fall Apart*. New York: Fawcett Crest–Ballantine, 1959.

———. "Thoughts on the African Novel." Achebe, *Morning* 49–54.

———. *The Trouble with Nigeria*. Enugu: Fourth Dimension, 1983; London: Heinemann, 1985.

————. "Viewpoint." *Times Literary Supplement* 1 Feb. 1980: 113. Rpt. as "Impediments to Dialogue between North and South" in Achebe, *Hopes* 14–19.

————. "The Writer and His Community." Achebe, *Hopes* 32–41.

Afigbo, A. E. "On the Threshold of Igbo History: Review of Thurstan Shaw's *Igbo-Ukwu.*" *Conch* 3.2 (1971): 205–18.

————. *Ropes of Sand: Studies in Igbo History and Culture.* Ibadan: University; London: Oxford UP, 1981.

————. *The Warrant Chiefs: Indirect Rule in Southeastern Nigeria, 1891–1929.* London: Longman, 1972.

Aguolu, Christian Chukwunedu. *Nigeria: A Comprehensive Bibliography in the Humanities and Social Sciences, 1900–1971.* Boston: Hall, 1973.

Allott, Miriam. *Novelists on the Novel.* London: Routledge, 1959.

Amadi, Elechi. *Ethics in Nigerian Culture.* London: Heinemann, 1982.

Anafulu, Joseph C. *The Ibo-Speaking Peoples of Southern Nigeria: A Selected Annotated List of Writings, 1627–1970.* Munich: Kraus, 1981.

————. "Igbo Life and Art: Igbo Language and Literature. Selected Bibliographies." *Conch* 3.2 (1971): 181–203.

Anene, J. C. *Southern Nigeria in Transition, 1885–1906: Theory and Practice in a Colonial Protectorate.* Cambridge: Cambridge UP, 1966.

Asturias, Miguel Angel. *Men of Maize.* Trans. Gerald Martin. New York: Seymour Lawrence–Delacorte, 1975. Trans. of *Hombres de maíz.* Ed. Gerald Martin. Paris: Editions Klincksieck; Mexico City: Fondo de Cultura Económica, 1981.

————. "Uspantán e Ilóm." Asturias, *Hombres* 245–46.

Attwell, David. "Chinua Achebe: *Things Fall Apart.*" *Explorations in the Novel: A Student's Guide to Setworks at South African Universities.* Ed. C. H. Muller. Johannesburg: Macmillan, 1984. 115–23.

Awoonor, Kofi. *The Breast of the Earth: A Survey of the History, Culture, and Literature of Africa South of the Sahara.* Garden City: Anchor-Doubleday, 1975.

Awoyinfa, Michael. "Chinua Achebe: *Things Fall Apart* Was Nearly Stolen from Me." *Sunday Concord Magazine* 6 Nov. 1983: i, v, xi.

Ayandele, E. A. *The Missionary Impact on Modern Nigeria, 1842–1914: A Political and Social Analysis.* Harlow: Longman, 1966.

Ayisi, Eric O. *An Introduction to the Study of African Culture.* London: Heinemann, 1972.

Bakhtin, M. M. *The Dialogic Imagination: Four Essays.* Trans. Caryl Emerson and Michael Holquist. Austin: U of Texas P, 1981.

Barthes, Roland. "The Death of the Author." *Image-Music-Text.* Trans. Stephen Heath. New York: Hill, 1977. 142–48.

Basden, G. T. *Niger Ibos.* London: Seeley, 1938; London: Cass, 1966.

Belsey, Catherine. *Critical Practice.* London: Methuen, 1980.

Benjamin, Walter. "Theses on the Philosophy of History." *Illuminations.* Trans. Harry Zohn. London: Cape, 1970. 255–66.

Bessinger, Jess B., Jr., and Robert F. Yeager, eds. *Approaches to Teaching* Beowulf. New York: MLA, 1984.

Bohannan, Paul, and Philip Curtin. *Africa and Africans.* Prospect Heights: Waveland, 1988.

Book of Chilam Balam of Chumayel. Ed. Ralph L. Roys. Norman: U of Oklahoma P, 1973.

Booth, James. *Writers and Politics in Nigeria.* London: Hodder, 1981.

Bovill, E. W. *Caravans of the Old Sahara.* London: Intl. Inst. of African Languages and Cultures, 1933.

Brantlinger, Patrick. "*Heart of Darkness*: Anti-Imperialism, Racism, or Impressionism?" *Criticism* 27 (1985): 363–85.

Burns, Alan Cuthbert. "Nigeria: History." *Encyclopaedia Britannica.* 1969.

Burns, E. Bradford. *Latin America: A Concise Interpretive History.* 4th ed. Englewood Cliffs: Prentice, 1986.

Cabral, Amilcar. *Return to the Source: Selected Speeches by Amilcar Cabral.* Ed. African Information Service. New York: Monthly Review, 1973.

———. *Unity and Struggle: Speeches and Writings.* Trans. Michael Wolfers. London: Heinemann, 1980.

Carroll, David. *Chinua Achebe.* New York: Twayne, 1970. 2nd ed., London: Macmillan; New York: St. Martin's, 1980.

Cartey, Wilfred. *Whispers from a Continent: Writings from Contemporary Black Africa.* New York: Random, 1969.

Cary, Joyce. *Mister Johnson.* London: Gollancz, 1939.

Césaire, Aimé. *Discourse on Colonialism.* Trans. Joan Pinkham. New York: Monthly Review, 1972.

Chametzky, Jules. *Our Decentralized Literature.* Amherst: U of Massachusetts P, 1986.

Chinweizu. "An Interview with Chinua Achebe (Nsukka, 20 January 1981)." *Okike* 20 (1981): 19–32.

Conrad, Joseph. *Heart of Darkness.* Ed. Robert Kimbrough. New York: Norton, 1963.

Cook, David. *African Literature: A Critical View.* London: Longman, 1977.

Cott, Jonathan. "Chinua Achebe: At the Crossroads." *Parabola* 6.2 (1981): 30–39. Rpt. in *Pipers at the Gates of Dawn: The Wisdom of Children's Literature.* Ed. Cott. New York: McGraw, 1985. 161–92.

Coulibaly, Yédiéti Edouard. "Weeping Gods: A Study of Cultural Disintegration in James Baldwin's *Go Tell It on the Mountain* and Chinua Achebe's *Things Fall Apart.*" *Annales de l'Université d'Abidjan* 9D (1976): 531–42.

Coussy, Denise. *L'oeuvre de Chinua Achebe.* Paris: Présence Africaine, 1985.

Cronin, Jeremy. "A Tale of Why Tortoise Carries a Hut upon His Back." *Inside.* London: Cape, 1987. 103–04.

Crowder, Michael. *A Short History of Nigeria.* New York: Praeger, 1966.

Davidson, Basil. *A History of West Africa to the Nineteenth Century*. Garden City: Anchor-Doubleday, 1966.

——. *Old Africa Rediscovered*. London: Gollancz, 1959.

Derrida, Jacques. *Margins of Philosophy*. Trans. Alan Bass. Chicago: U of Chicago P, 1982.

Dike, K. Onwuka. *Trade and Politics in the Niger Delta, 1830–1835: An Introduction to the Economic and Political History of Nigeria*. Oxford: Clarendon–Oxford UP, 1956.

Doctorow, E. L. *Ragtime*. New York: Random, 1975.

Dreiser, Theodore. *Sister Carrie*. New York: Doubleday, 1900.

Duerden, Dennis. "Chinua Achebe." Duerden and Pieterse 9–11.

Duerden, Dennis, and Cosmo Pieterse, eds. *African Writers Talking: A Collection of Radio Interviews*. London: Heinemann Educational, 1972.

Edwards, Paul. "Editor's Introduction." Equiano vii–xix.

Egejuru, Phanuel Akubueze, ed. *Towards African Literary Independence: A Dialogue with Contemporary African Writers*. Westport: Greenwood, 1980.

Egudu, Romanus N. "Achebe and the Igbo Narrative Tradition." *Research in African Literatures* 12 (1981): 43–54.

Eko, Ebele. "Chinua Achebe and His Critics: Reception of His Novels in English and American Reviews." *Studies in Black Literature* 6.3 (1975): 14–20.

Ekwe-Ekwe, Herbert. "A Week-end of African Literature." *Guardian* 17 Aug. 1986: B8.

Emenyonu, Ernest. "Early Fiction in Igbo." *Research in African Literatures* 4 (1973): 7–20. Rev. and rpt. in Emenyonu, *Rise* 33–53, 155–61.

——. *The Rise of the Igbo Novel*. Ibadan: Oxford UP, 1978.

Emenyonu, Ernest, and Pat Emenyonu. "Achebe: Accountable to Our Society." *Africa Report* 17.5 (1972): 21, 23, 25–27.

Engels, Friedrich. "Letter to Minna Kautsky" and "Letter to Margaret Harkness." *Dramatic Theory and Criticism: Greeks to Grotowski*. Ed. Bernard F. Dukore. New York: Holt, 1974. 801–04.

Equiano, Olaudah. *Equiano's Travels: His Autobiography*. Ed. Paul Edwards. London: Heinemann Educational, 1967.

Fanon, Frantz. *A Dying Colonialism*. New York: Grove, 1967.

——. *The Wretched of the Earth*. London: Penguin, 1967.

Forde, C. D., and G. I. Jones. *The Ibo and Ibibio-Speaking Peoples of South-eastern Nigeria*. London: International African Inst., 1950.

Forster, E. M. *A Passage to India*. London: Arnold, 1924.

Foucault, Michel. "What Is an Author?" *Textual Strategies: Perspectives in Poststructuralist Criticism*. Ed. Josué V. Harari. Ithaca: Cornell UP, 1979. 141–60.

Fraser, Robert. "A Note on Okonkwo's Suicide." *Kunapipi* 1.1 (1979): 108–13. Rpt. in *Obsidian* 6.1–2 (1980): 33–37.

Fuentes, Carlos. *La nueva novela hispanoamericana*. Mexico City: Joaquín Mortiz, 1969.

Gates, Henry Louis, Jr., ed. *Black Literature and Literary Theory*. New York: Methuen, 1984.

Gibaldi, Joseph, ed. *Approaches to Teaching Chaucer's* Canterbury Tales. New York: MLA, 1980.

Gikandi, Simon. *Reading the African Novel*. London: Heinemann, 1987.

Githae-Mugo, Micere. *Visions of Africa: The Fiction of Chinua Achebe, Margaret Laurence, Elspeth Huxley, and Ngugi wa Thiong'o*. Nairobi: Kenya Literature Bureau, 1978.

Gleason, Judith. *This Africa: Novels by West Africans in English and French*. Evanston: Northwestern UP, 1965.

Goonetilleke, D. C. R. A. *Developing Countries in British Fiction*. London: Macmillan, 1977.

Gowda, H. H. Anniah. "Ahmed Ali's *Twilight in Delhi* (1940), and Achebe's *Things Fall Apart* (1958)." *Literary Half-Yearly* 21.1 (1980): 11–18.

Gramsci, Antonio. "Observations on Folklore." *Communication and Class Struggle*. Vol. 2. Ed. A. Mattelart and S. Siegelaub. 3 vols. New York: International General, 1983. 71–75.

Granqvist, Raoul. "Chinua Achebe's Language: An Examination of Views." *A Sense of Place: Essays in Post-colonial Literatures*. Ed. Britta Olinder. Gothenburg: English Dept., Gothenburg U, 1984. 177–89.

———. "The Early Swedish Reviews of Chinua Achebe's *Things Fall Apart* and *A Man of the People*." *Research in African Literatures* 15 (1984): 394–404.

Green, M. M. *Ibo Village Affairs*. London: Sidgwick, 1947; London: Cass, 1964.

———. *Land Tenure in an Ibo Village in South-eastern Nigeria*. London: Lund, 1941.

Green, Martin. *Dreams of Adventure, Deeds of Empire*. London: Routledge, 1980.

Griffeths, Gareth. *A Double Exile: African and West Indian Writing between Two Cultures*. London: Boyars, 1978.

———. "Language and Action in the Novels of Chinua Achebe." *African Literature Today* 5 (1971): 88–105.

Guibert, Rita, ed. *Seven Voices: Seven Latin American Writers Talk to Rita Guibert*. Trans. Frances Partridge. New York: Knopf, 1973.

Gunner, Elizabeth. *A Handbook for Teaching African Literature*. London: Heinemann Educational, 1984.

Guzmán-Böckler, Carlos, and Jean Loup Herbert. *Guatemala: Una interpretación histórico-social*. 5th ed. Mexico City: Siglo XXI, 1975.

Hall, R. N. *Great Zimbabwe*. London: Methuen, 1905.

Harris, Wilson. "The Frontier on Which *Heart of Darkness* Stands." *Research in African Literatures* 12 (1981): 86–93. Rpt. in *Explorations: A Selection of Talks and Articles, 1966–1981*. By Harris. Mundelstrup, Den.: Dangaroo, 1981.

Hastings, Adrian. *African Christianity*. New York: Harper, 1977.

Hawkins, Hunt. "The Issue of Racism in *Heart of Darkness.*" *Conradiana* 14 (1982): 163–71.

Herdeck, Donald E. *African Authors: A Companion to Black African Writing; Vol. 1: 1300–1973.* Washington: Black Orpheus, 1973.

Heywood, Christopher. *Chinua Achebe's* Things Fall Apart: *A Critical View.* Ed. Yolande Cantù. London: Collins, 1985.

———. "Surface and Symbol in *Things Fall Apart.*" *Journal of the Nigerian English Studies Association* 2 (1967): 41–45.

Hobsbawm, Eric. "Introduction: Inventing Traditions." *The Invention of Tradition.* Ed. Eric Hobsbawm and Terence Ranger. Cambridge: Cambridge UP, 1983. 1–14.

Howe, Susanne. *Novels of Empire.* New York: Columbia UP, 1949.

Innes, C. L. *Chinua Achebe.* Cambridge: Cambridge UP, 1990.

———. "Language, Poetry and Doctrine in *Things Fall Apart.*" Innes and Lindfors 111–25.

Innes, C. L., and Bernth Lindfors, eds. *Critical Perspectives on Chinua Achebe.* Washington: Three Continents, 1978; London: Heinemann, 1979.

Irele, Abiola. *The African Experience in Literature and Ideology.* London: Heinemann, 1981.

———. "The Tragic Conflict in Achebe's Novels." *Black Orpheus* 17 (1965): 24–32.

Isichei, Elizabeth. Rev. of *Achebe's World,* by Robert M. Wren. *Journal of African History* 24 (1983): 414–15.

———. *A History of the Igbo People.* London: Macmillan, 1976.

———. *The Ibo People and the Europeans: The Genesis of a Relationship—to 1906.* London: Faber, 1973.

Ita, Nduntuei O. *Bibliography of Nigeria: A Survey of Anthropological and Linguistic Writings from the Earliest Times to 1966.* London: Cass, 1971.

Iyasere, Solomon O. "Narrative Techniques in *Things Fall Apart.*" *New Letters* 40.3 (1974): 73–93.

Jabbi, Bu-Buakei. "Fire and Transition in *Things Fall Apart.*" *Obsidian* 1.3 (1975): 22–36. Rpt. in Innes and Lindfors 93–110.

Jahn, Janheinz. *A History of Neo-African Literature: Writing in Two Continents.* Trans. Oliver Coburn and Ursula Lehrburger. London: Faber, 1968; New York: Grove, 1969.

———. *Muntu: An Outline of the New African Culture.* Trans. Marjorie Grene. London: Faber; New York: Grove, 1961.

Jahn, Janheinz, Ulla Schild, and Almut Nordmann. *Who's Who in African Literature: Biographies, Works, Commentaries.* Tübingen: Erdmann, 1972.

JanMohamed, Abdul R. *Manichean Aesthetics: The Politics of Literature in Colonial Africa.* Amherst: U of Massachusetts P, 1983.

———. "Sophisticated Primitivism: The Syncretism of Oral and Literate Modes in Achebe's *Things Fall Apart.*" *Ariel* 15.4 (1984): 19–39.

Jervis, Steven. "Tradition and Change in Hardy and Achebe." *Black Orpheus* 2.5–6 (1971): 31–38.

Jeyifo, Biodun. *Contemporary Nigerian Literature: A Retrospective and Prospective Exploration*. Lagos: Nigeria Magazine, 1985.

Jones, Eldred. "Language and Theme in *Things Fall Apart*." *Review of English Literature* 5.4 (1964): 39–43.

Kane, Cheikh Hamidou. *Ambiguous Adventure*. African Writers Series. London: Heinemann, 1972.

Killam, G. D. *Africa in English Fiction, 1874–1939*. Ibadan: Ibadan UP, 1968.

———, ed. *African Writers on African Writing*. London: Heinemann; Evanston: Northwestern UP, 1973.

———. *The Novels of Chinua Achebe*. London: Heinemann; New York: Africana, 1969. Rev. and rpt. as *The Writings of Chinua Achebe*. London: Heinemann, 1977.

Kipling, Rudyard. *Rudyard Kipling's Verse: Definitive Edition*. London: Hodder, 1940.

Kirk-Greene, A. H. M., ed. *Lugard and the Amalgamation of Nigeria: A Documentary Record*. London: Cass, 1968.

Knipp, Thomas R. "Myth, History, and the Poetry of Kofi Awoonor." *African Literature Today* 11 (1980): 39–61.

Kronenfeld, J. Z. "The 'Communalistic' African and the 'Individualistic' Westerner: Some Comments on Misleading Generalizations in Western Criticism of Soyinka and Achebe." *Research in African Literatures* 6 (1975): 199–225.

Kuesgen, Reinhardt. "Conrad and Achebe: Aspects of the Novel." *World Literature Written in English* 24 (1984): 27–33.

Kutzinski, Vera. "The Logic of Wings: Gabriel García Márquez and Afro-American Literature." *Latin American Literary Review* 13.25 (1985): 133–46.

Larson, Charles R. *The Emergence of African Fiction*. Bloomington: Indiana UP, 1971.

———. "The Film Version of *Things Fall Apart*." *Africana Journal* 13 (1982): 104–10.

Last, Brian W. "Literary Reactions to Colonialism: A Comparative Study of Joyce Cary, Chinua Achebe, and John Updike." *World Literature Written in English* 22 (1983): 151–70.

Laurence, Margaret. *Long Drums and Cannons: Nigerian Dramatists and Novelists, 1952–1966*. London: Macmillan, 1968; New York: Praeger, 1969.

Lawson, William. *The Western Scar: The Theme of the Been-to in West African Fiction*. Athens: Ohio UP, 1982.

Leith-Ross, Sylvia. *African Women: A Study of the Ibo of Nigeria*. London: Faber, 1939; London: Routledge, 1965.

Leonard, A. G. *The Lower Niger and Its Tribes*. London: Macmillan, 1906.

Levin, Harry. *Contexts of Criticism*. New York: Atheneum, 1963.

Lindfors, Bernth. *Black African Literature in English: A Guide to Information Sources*. Detroit: Gale, 1979.

―――. *Black African Literature in English: 1977–1981 Supplement*. New York: Africana, 1986.

―――. *Black African Literature in English, 1982–1986*. London: Zell, 1989.

―――. *Early Nigerian Literature*. New York: Africana, 1982.

―――. *Folklore in Nigerian Literature*. New York: Africana, 1973.

―――. "The Palm-Oil with Which Achebe's Words Are Eaten." *African Literature Today* 1 (1968): 3–18. Rpt. in Innes and Lindfors 47–66.

Lindfors, Bernth, Ian Munro, Richard Priebe, and Reinhard Sander, eds. *Palaver: Interviews with Five African Writers in Texas*. Austin: African and Afro-American Research Inst., U of Texas, 1974.

Lugard, F. D. "The Dual Mandate in British Tropical Africa." *Colonial Rule in Africa: Readings from Primary Sources*. Ed. Bruce Fetter. Madison: U of Wisconsin P, 1979. 96–98.

Lukács, Georg. *Essays on Realism*. London: Lawrence, 1980.

Mahood, M. M. *The Colonial Encounter: A Reading of Six Novels*. London: Collings, 1977.

Mannoni, O. *Prospero and Caliban*. New York: Praeger, 1964.

Mbiti, John. *African Religions and Philosophy*. London: Heinemann, 1969.

―――. *Introduction to African Religion*. London: Heinemann, 1975.

McDougall, Russell. "Okonkwo's Walk: A Choreography of *Things Fall Apart*." *Wasafiri* 3 (1985): 12–15. Rpt. in *World Literature Written in English* 26 (1986): 24–33.

McEwen, Neil. *Africa and the Novel*. London: Macmillan; Atlantic Highlands: Humanities, 1983.

Meek, C. K. *Law and Authority in a Nigerian Tribe*. London: Oxford UP, 1937.

Melone, Thomas. *Chinua Achebe et la tragédie de l'histoire*. Paris: Présence Africaine, 1973.

Memmi, Albert. *The Colonizer and the Colonized*. London: Souvenir, 1974.

Meyers, Jeffrey. *Fiction and the Colonial Experience*. Ipswich: Boydell, 1973.

Moore, Gerald. *Twelve African Writers*. Bloomington: Indiana UP, 1980.

Moorehead, Alan. *The Fatal Impact*. London: Hamilton, 1966.

Morell, Karen L., ed. *In Person: Achebe, Awoonor, and Soyinka at the University of Washington*. Seattle: African Studies Program, Inst. for Comparative and Foreign Area Studies, U of Washington, 1975.

Morris, Patricia. "The Politics of Language." *African Concord* 14 Aug. 1986: 19–21.

Moyers, Bill. "Chinua Achebe: Nigerian Novelist." *A World of Ideas*. Ed. Betty Sue Flowers. New York: Doubleday, 1989. 333–44.

Mphahlele, Ezekiel. *The African Image*. London: Faber, 1962; rev. ed., 1974.

Mudimbe, V. Y. *The Invention of Africa: Gnosis, Philosophy, and the Order of Knowledge*. Bloomington: Indiana UP, 1988.

―――. "Where Is the Real Thing?: Psychoanalysis and African Mythical Narratives." *Cahiers d'études africaines* 107–08 (1987): 311–27.

Nair, Kannan K. *Politics and Society in South Eastern Nigeria 1841–1906: A Study of Power, Diplomacy, and Commerce in Old Calabar.* London: Cass, 1972.

Ndibe, Okey, and C. Don Adinuba. "Africa Is Unstable"; "Nigeria Has Not Yet Been Founded"; "There Are Oppressors"; "Not a Matter of Noise." *African Guardian* 17 July 1986: 42; 24 July 1986: 34; 31 July 1986: 38; 7 Aug. 1986: 40.

Ngara, Emmanuel. *Art and Ideology in the African Novel.* London: Heinemann, 1985.

Niane, Djibril T. *Sundiata.* Ed. G. D. Pickett. London: Longman, 1965.

Njaka, Mazi E. N. *Igbo Political Culture.* Evanston: Northwestern UP, 1974.

Njoku, Benedict Chiaka. *The Four Novels of Chinua Achebe: A Critical Study.* New York: Lang, 1984.

Nkosi, Lewis. "Conversation with Chinua Achebe." *Africa Report* 9.7 (1964): 19–21. Rpt. in Duerden and Pieterse 3–6.

Nnolim, Charles. "Achebe's *Things Fall Apart*: An Igbo National Epic." *Modern Black Literature.* Ed. Okechukwu S. Mezu. New York: Black Academy, 1971. 55–60.

Obiechina, Emmanuel. *Culture, Tradition, and Society in the West African Novel.* Cambridge: Cambridge UP, 1975.

———. "Problem of Language in African Writing: The Example of the Novel." *Conch* 5.1–2 (1973): 11–28.

———. "Structure and Significance in Achebe's *Things Fall Apart*." *English in Africa* 2.2 (1975): 39–44.

Ogbaa, Kalu. "A Cultural Note on Okonkwo's Suicide." *Kunapipi* 3.2 (1981): 126–34.

———. *Folkways in Chinua Achebe's Novels.* Oguta: Zim, 1990; Trenton: Africa World, forthcoming.

———. "An Interview with Chinua Achebe." *Research in African Literatures* 12 (1981): 1–13.

Okafor, Clement A. "Igbo Narrative Tradition and the Novels of Chinua Achebe: Transition from Oral to Written Literature." *Evolution of the Novel.* Ed. Zoran Konstantinovic, Eva Kushner, and Béla Köpeczi. 4 vols. Proc. of the Congress of the International Comparative Literature Association. Innsbruck: Instituts für Sprachwissenschaft der Universität Innsbruck, 1982. 4: 483–87.

Okoye, Emmanuel Meziemadu. *The Traditional Religion and Its Encounter with Christianity in Achebe's Novels.* New York: Lang, 1987.

Okpu, B. *Chinua Achebe: A Bibliography.* Lagos: Libriservice, 1984.

Oliver, Roland, and J. D. Fage. *A Short History of Africa.* Harmondsworth: Penguin, 1968.

Olney, James. *Tell Me Africa: An Approach to African Literature.* Princeton: Princeton UP, 1973.

Ottenberg, Simon. "The Present State of Igbo Studies." *Journal of the Historical Society of Nigeria* 2.2 (1961): 211–30.

———. "Supplementary Bibliography on the Ibo-Speaking Peoples of South-eastern Nigeria." *African Studies* 14 (1955): 63–85.

Owomoyela, Oyekan. *African Literatures: An Introduction*. Waltham: Crossroads, 1979.

———. "Chinua Achebe on the Individual in Society." *Journal of African Studies* 12 (1985): 53–65.

Page, James A., and Jae Min Roh, comps. *Selected Black American, African, and Caribbean Authors: A Bio-Bibliography*. Littleton: Libraries Unlimited, 1985.

Palmer, Eustace. "Character and Society in Achebe's *Things Fall Apart*." *Literary Half-Yearly* 22.1 (1981): 13–27.

———. *The Growth of the African Novel*. London: Heinemann, 1979.

———. *An Introduction to the African Novel*. London: Heinemann; New York: Africana, 1972.

Parry, Benita. *Delusions and Discoveries: Studies on India in the British Imagination, 1880–1930*. London: Allen Lane, 1972.

Perham, Marjory. *Native Administration in Nigeria*. London: Oxford UP, 1937.

Peters, Jonathan. *A Dance of Masks: Senghor, Achebe, Soyinka*. Washington: Three Continents, 1978.

Popol Vuh: The Definitive Edition of the Mayan Book of the Dawn of Life and the Glories of the Gods and Kings. Trans. Dennis Tedlock. New York: Simon, 1985.

Priebe, Richard K. "Fate and Divine Justice in *Things Fall Apart*." *Neo-African Literature and Culture: Essays in Memory of Janheinz Jahn*. Ed. Bernth Lindfors and Ulla Schild. Wiesbaden: Heymann, 1976. 159–66.

———. *Myth, Realism, and the West African Writer*. Trenton: Africa World, 1986.

Ramkrishnan, E. V. "The Novel of Memory and the Third World Reality: Gabriel Márquez and Chinua Achebe." *Indian Readings in Commonwealth Literature*. Ed. G. S. Amur et al. New Delhi: Sterling, 1985. 124–31.

Raskin, Jonah. *The Mythology of Imperialism*. New York: Random, 1971.

Ravenscroft, Arthur. *Chinua Achebe*. Harlow: Longman, 1969; 1977.

Ridley, Hugh. *Images of Imperial Rule*. London: Croom Helm, 1983.

Robertson, P. J. M. "*Things Fall Apart* and *Heart of Darkness*: A Creative Dialogue." *International Fiction Review* 7 (1980): 106–11.

Rodney, Walter. *How Europe Underdeveloped Africa*. Washington: Howard UP, 1974.

Roscoe, Adrian. *Mother Is Gold: A Study of West African Literature*. Cambridge: Cambridge UP, 1971.

Said, Edward W. *Orientalism*. New York: Random, 1979.

Sandison, Alan. *The Wheel of Empire: A Study of the Imperial Idea in Some Late Nineteenth- and Early Twentieth-Century Fiction*. London: Macmillan; New York: St. Martin's, 1967.

Sarvan, C. P. "Racism and the *Heart of Darkness*." *International Fiction Review* 7 (1980): 6–10.

Scheub, Harold. "When a Man Fails Alone." *Présence africaine* 74 (1970): 61–89.

Schmidt, Nancy. *Sub-Saharan African Films and Filmmakers: An Annotated Bibliography*. London: Zell, 1988.

Shaw, Thurstan. *Igbo-Ukwu: An Account of Archaeological Discoveries in Eastern Nigeria*. 2 vols. Evanston: Northwestern UP, 1970.

———. *Unearthing Igbo-Ukwu: Archaeological Discoveries in Eastern Nigeria*. Ibadan: Oxford UP, 1977.

Shelton, Austin J. "The 'Palm-Oil' of Language: Proverbs in Chinua Achebe's Novels." *Modern Language Quarterly* 30 (1969): 86–111.

Snow, C. P. *The Realists*. New York: Macmillan, 1978.

"Southern Nigeria, September–December 1905. Offices: Admiralty and Crown Agents." Colonial Office file 520/32. Public Record Office, London.

"Southern Nigeria Dispatches." Colonial Office file 520/35. Public Record Office, London.

Soyinka, Wole. *Myth, Literature, and the African World*. Cambridge: Cambridge UP, 1978.

Stallknecht, Newton. Foreword. Larson, *Emergence* iv–xi.

Stock, A. G. "Yeats and Achebe." *Journal of Commonwealth Literature* 5 (1968): 105–11.

Taiwo, Oladele. *Culture and the Nigerian Novel*. London: Macmillan; New York: St. Martin's, 1976.

———. *An Introduction to West African Literature*. London: Nelson; New York: Humanities, 1967.

Talbot, Percy Amaury. *In the Shadow of the Bush*. London: Heinemann, 1912.

Thomas, Northcote W. *Anthropological Report on the Ibo-Speaking Peoples of Nigeria*. London: Harrison, 1913–14; New York: Negro UP, 1969.

Thompson, Stith. *Motif Index of Folk-Literature*. Bloomington: Indiana UP, 1932–36.

Timberg, Bernard. "Chinua Achebe's *Things Fall Apart* and Chaim Potok's *The Chosen*." *Kiabàrà* 2 (1979): 102–28.

Trigona, Prospero. *La maledizione del serpenta: Saggio sulla narrativa di Chinua Achebe*. Milan: Edizioni Universitarie Jaca, 1989.

Tucker, Martin. *Africa in Modern Literature: A Survey of Contemporary Writing in English*. New York: Ungar, 1967.

Turkington, Kate. *Chinua Achebe:* Things Fall Apart. London: Arnold, 1977.

Turnbull, Colin. *The Lonely African*. London: Chatto, 1963; New York: Simon, 1968.

Tutuola, Amos. *The Palm-Wine Drinkard*. London: Faber, 1952.

Uchendu, Victor C. *The Igbo of Southeast Nigeria*. New York: Holt, 1965.

Ugah, Ada. *In the Beginning . . . : Chinua Achebe at Work*. Ibadan: Heinemann Educational, 1990.

Umeasiegbu, Rems Nna. *Words Are Sweet: Igbo Stories and Storytelling*. Leiden: Brill, 1982.

Uwechie, Cele, Moses Ugwoke, et al. *Chinua Achebe: A Bio-bibliography*. Nsukka: Faculty of Arts, U of Nigeria, 1990.

Vincent, Theo. "Register in Achebe." *Journal of the Nigerian English Studies Association* 6 (1974): 95–106.

Wattie, Nelson. "The Community as Protagonist in the Novels of Chinua Achebe and Witi Ihimaera." *Individual and Community in Commonwealth Literature.* Ed. Daniel Massa. Msida: U of Malta P, 1979. 69–74.

Watts, Cedric. " 'A Bloody Racist': About Achebe's View of Conrad." *Yearbook of English Studies* 13 (1983): 196–209.

Wauthier, Claude. *The Literature and Thought of Modern Africa.* London: Heinemann, 1978.

Weinstock, Donald J. "The Two Swarms of Locusts: Judgement by Indirection in *Things Fall Apart.*" *Studies in Black Literature* 2.1 (1971): 14–19.

Weinstock, Donald J., and Cathy Ramadan. "Symbolic Structure in *Things Fall Apart.*" *Critique* 11 (1969): 33–41. Rpt. in Innes and Lindfors 126–34.

West, Cornel. "Demystifying Theory: The Impact of Race, Gender, and Class in Cultural Studies." U of Texas, Austin, 24 Apr. 1989.

Williams, Chancellor. *The Destruction of Black Civilization.* Chicago: Third World, 1974.

Williams, Philip G. "A Comparative Approach to Afro-American and Neo-African Novels: Ellison and Achebe." *Studies in Black Literature* 7.1 (1976): 15–18.

Winters, Marjorie. "Morning Yet on Judgement Day: The Critics of Chinua Achebe." *Journal of the Literary Society of Nigeria* 1 (1981): 26–39. Rpt. in *When the Drumbeat Changes.* Ed. Carolyn A. Parker et al. Washington: Three Continents, 1981. 169–85.

———. "An Objective Approach to Achebe's Style." *Research in African Literatures* 12 (1981): 55–68.

Woolfson, Karen. "Writers in Conversation." *African Concord* 14 Aug. 1986: 18–19.

Worsley, Peter. *The Three Worlds: Culture and World Development.* London: Weidenfeld, 1984.

Wren, Robert M. *Achebe's World: The Historical and Cultural Context of the Novels of Chinua Achebe.* Washington: Three Continents; Harlow: Longman, 1980.

———. *Chinua Achebe:* Things Fall Apart. London: Longman, 1980.

Wynter, Sylvia. "History, Ideology, and the Reinvention of the Past in Achebe's *Things Fall Apart* and Laye's *The Dark Child.*" *Minority Voices* 2.1 (1978): 43–61.

Yankson, Kofi E. *Chinua Achebe's Novels: A Sociolinguistic Perspective.* Uruowulu-Obosi, Nigeria: Pacific, 1990.

Zell, Hans M., Carol Bundy, and Virginia Coulon, eds. *A New Reader's Guide to African Literature.* 2nd ed. London: Heinemann; New York: Africana, 1983.

Zins, Henryk. *Joseph Conrad and Africa.* Nairobi: Kenya Literature Bureau, 1982.

INDEX

Modern Language Association of America
Approaches to Teaching World Literature
Joseph Gibaldi, series editor

Medieval English Drama. Ed. Richard K. Emmerson. 1990.

Melville's Moby-Dick. Ed. Martin Bickman. 1985.

Metaphysical Poets. Ed. Sidney Gottlieb. 1990.

Miller's Death of a Salesman. Ed. Matthew C. Roudané. 1995.

Milton's Paradise Lost. Ed. Galbraith M. Crump. 1986.

Molière's Tartuffe *and Other Plays*. Ed. James F. Gaines and Michael S. Koppisch. 1995.

Momaday's The Way to Rainy Mountain. Ed. Kenneth M. Roemer. 1988.

Montaigne's Essays. Ed. Patrick Henry. 1994.

Novels of Toni Morrison. Ed. Nellie Y. McKay and Kathryn Earle. 1997.

Murasaki Shikibu's The Tale of Genji. Ed. Edward Kamens. 1993.

Pope's Poetry. Ed. Wallace Jackson and R. Paul Yoder. 1993.

Shakespeare's King Lear. Ed. Robert H. Ray. 1986.

Shakespeare's The Tempest *and Other Late Romances*. Ed. Maurice Hunt. 1992.

Shelley's Frankenstein. Ed. Stephen C. Behrendt. 1990.

Shelley's Poetry. Ed. Spencer Hall. 1990.

Sir Gawain and the Green Knight. Ed. Miriam Youngerman Miller and Jane Chance. 1986.

Spenser's Faerie Queene. Ed. David Lee Miller and Alexander Dunlop. 1994.

Sterne's Tristram Shandy. Ed. Melvyn New. 1989.

Swift's Gulliver's Travels. Ed. Edward J. Rielly. 1988.

Thoreau's Walden *and Other Works*. Ed. Richard J. Schneider. 1996.

Voltaire's Candide. Ed. Renée Waldinger. 1987.

Whitman's Leaves of Grass. Ed. Donald D. Kummings. 1990.

Wordsworth's Poetry. Ed. Spencer Hall, with Jonathan Ramsey. 1986.

Wright's Native Son. Ed. James A. Miller. 1997.